A. E. ANGEL

DEAD WHISPERS

GHOSTLY EVPs

audio CD inside

Schiffer Publishing Ltd

4880 Lower Valley Road • Atglen, PA 19310

Designed by Danielle D. Farmer
Cover Design by Justin Watkinson
Type set in Bad Deni/Helvetica Neue Lt Pro
ISBN: 978-0-7643-4236-3
Printed in China

Schiffer Books are available at special discounts for bulk purchases for sales promotions or premiums. Special editions, including personalized covers, corporate imprints, and excerpts can be created in large quantities for special needs. For more information contact the publisher:

Published by Schiffer Publishing, Ltd.
4880 Lower Valley Road
Atglen, PA 19310
Phone: (610) 593-1777; Fax: (610) 593-2002
E-mail: Info@schifferbooks.com

For the largest selection of fine reference books on this and related subjects, please visit our website at **www.schifferbooks.com**
We are always looking for people to write books on new and related subjects. If you have an idea for a book, please contact us at proposals@schifferbooks.com

This book may be purchased from the publisher.
Please try your bookstore first.
You may write for a free catalog.

In Europe, Schiffer books are distributed by
Bushwood Books
6 Marksbury Ave.
Kew Gardens
Surrey TW9 4JF England
Phone: 44 (0) 20 8392 8585; Fax: 44 (0) 20 8392 9876
E-mail: info@bushwoodbooks.co.uk
Website: www.bushwoodbooks.co.uk

CD, text and photos by author unless otherwise noted

Front Cover photo: "Family Affair." *Courtesy Crystal Washington, WCG*
Back Cover Photo: Oak Grove Cemetery, New Bedford, MA

DEDICATION

DEAD WHISPERS IS DEDICATED TO ALL THE PEOPLE
WHO HAVE TOUCHED MY LIFE, BOTH LIVING AND DEAD.

BIG THANKS TO MWB; I DON'T KNOW IF I COULD HAVE
DONE THIS WITHOUT YOUR LOVE AND SUPPORT!

TO MY SONS, WHEN YOU LOOK THROUGH YOUR EYES,
NEVER FORGET TO SEE WITH YOUR HEART!

ROCK ON STILETTO GALS!

HOME IS WHERE THE HEART IS;
THANKS GOING OUT TO THE CITY OF NEW BEDFORD!

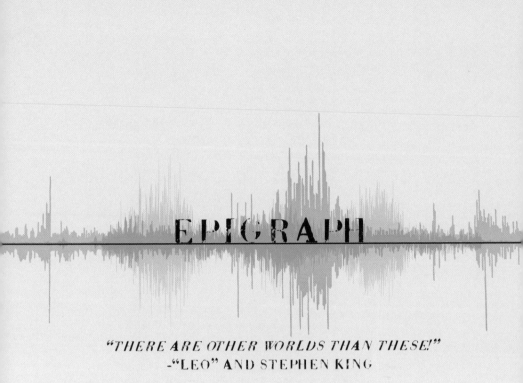

EPIGRAPH

"THERE ARE OTHER WORLDS THAN THESE!"
-"LEO" AND STEPHEN KING

CONTENTS

INTRODUCTION

Ever since I was a little girl, things have happened to me that I couldn't explain. As the years went by and strange phenomena kept happening to me, I realized that the best place for me to be was in the paranormal field. So, for the past twenty-seven years, I have been doing what I seem to do best. I talk to dead people. And dead people talk back to me.

By 2004, I was actively looking for paranormal women who shared some of my traits. I had an idea that if you put people who ghosts are attracted to into the paranormal field, ghosts would come. And ghosts would talk. I believed that if I pushed the boundaries of known science, more answers would come.

Though I haven't come closer to proving the existence of life after death, I have recorded some compelling evidence of human spirits who have passed on to the other side. Each of these spirits that I've met have touched me in some way—shown me that the petty little things we living humans are so concerned about don't really matter much in the greater scheme of things. Because of the dead, I have learned just how important life really is...that death is just a natural part of life, and that it doesn't necessarily mean the end of our souls.

Most people would think that my life is made up of a number of coincidences. But I'm not so sure I believe that. Coincidence or not, the events of my life have led me to where I am today. Days before the man I loved died, he told me something I could never forget. As we lay together, gazing up at the stars, he told me that there are other worlds than this. He told me he believed that what we did in this life was the basis for what would happen to us after we died. That if we did our best and did good things, we would go on to a better world than this. Years later, I read those very same words in Stephen King's novel, *The Gunslinger*. I don't believe it was a coincidence that two people who had so much influence over my life had told me the exact same thing. These words have become the basis for many of my ideas that I apply to the paranormal. For I've come to believe that there are many worlds, many dimensions that exist that we can not see as we live our human lives.

How could two totally different men have such an influence on my life, on what I've become? One that I knew and loved and died saving my life; the other a person I'd never met, but even so, had great influence over who I am today. Let me explain.

A long time ago, there was a young girl who lived in fear. She didn't understand the paranormal events that were a regular part of her life. She believed something was wrong with her and wished with all her heart that she could be just like everyone else. It took a man, who later became a spiritual eagle to this girl, to show her that there was something special about her. That she was worth something after all, and that she was worthy of great love. He taught her to care not for others, but for herself. He showed her that in order to love fully, one must first love one's self. It took that girl years to understand his sacrifice, that by giving his own life, he had saved her and taught her things she never thought she'd know. Though he no longer exists in this world, he is out there still, flying, waiting for her.

Through all of this, other lessons were being taught. Lessons I never understood at the time, but which were learned in the strangest of ways. For in his own way, Stephen King became a spiritual father to me. He created characters that lived through worse events than I ever had. And through his characters, both evil and good, he showed me

Massachusetts has more cemeteries than any other state. Though the high number of burial grounds is due to small family plots dotting the landscape high and low, New Bedford has numerous large and small resting places that date back hundreds of years. Oak Grove Cemetery, New Bedford, MA.
Courtesy of Crystal Washington, WCG

what I wanted to be some day. He showed me that it's all right to be frightened, terrified by events I have no control over, but even so, I can still do the right thing. That to follow my heart wasn't really such a bad practice. In his own way, without even knowing he had done it, he confirmed some things for me. I can not even begin to describe how the world started turning when I read Leo's words in a Stephen King story that later became one of my favorite series of all time. For I do believe there was a message for me in these words, and that there *are* other worlds than this. And that when I step into the paranormal investigative field, I can reach out and touch upon these worlds and that these worlds reach back and touch me.

I believe that if I hadn't known, via these two very special and important men, I would not have the courage or determination to keep reaching out. To keep striving to teach people that we all matter. And that we all go on, even after death. Because of these two men touching my life in such ways, I am determined to teach everyone else that we do matter. What we do and how we feel does make us what we are. Though I lost the one I loved above all others when he saved my physical life in a terrible car accident on a rainy November night, I know he will always be with me. That I will see him again. Maybe it will be in this world, or maybe one of the others that I truly believe exist out there. Maybe we will visit them all. Coincidence? Circumstance? No, I don't think so. But what I *do* think is that all of this is just the natural journey of the human soul. A journey that each and every one of us has to take. A journey that I have come to think of as neverending, with many roads to travel, many paths to tread upon. To me, death is no longer an ending. It is just another beginning.

And so, I invite you to enter my world. A place in which the paranormal is an everyday event. An existence in which I travel to these other worlds, without ever leaving Earth. Where I call out and reach for the dead. Where the dead call out and reach for me.

What better time to take you on such a journey? Every day, without even knowing it, we tread upon the blood of the true owners of this country. The turmoil and illnesses, battles and wars, that were fought upon our soil are some of the bloodiest battles ever fought upon this country's lands. Native peoples all but disappeared, our forefathers fought and died, family tragedies occurred. Somehow, some way, many of the spirits of these people are still here. They still speak, they still touch us, they still manipulate this physical world we live in.

As I've searched for answers as to how this could possibly be, I've found myself caring for these spirits, these people who once were. And wondering: What holds them here to this place? Why do they stay on here? Why are they so willing to speak with us, the living? I can not tell you why. But I can tell you that they do just that. And I can invite you to read on, and meet these spirits who have come to earn a place in my heart.

As I introduce you to the spirits I've met over the years, Lizzie Borden herself, the members of a gentleman's club of yesterday, victims of murder and illness, I think you'll find yourself caring for them, too. For each and every one of these "ghosts," these people who have passed on to some other world, were once just like us. Living, breathing, loving, hurting...and they all have a story to tell. I hope I can tell their stories well, that I make them proud, and that I have a place in their hearts, too. And as you read on, I hope that they will find a place in your heart as well!

Crystal and Luann enjoy perfect spring weather in Oak Grove Cemetery, New Bedford, Massachusetts, during a training session with WCG's newest member, Susan Swanbeck. *Courtesy Marc Pacheco, Independent Investigator*

LUANN JOLY/A. E. ANGEL FOUNDER/AUDIO

After years of experiencing the paranormal, I decided it was time to turn things around. If I couldn't escape the paranormal, well it wouldn't be able to escape me either. I began studying science and the paranormal sometime around 1985. As time went on, I discovered that this was where I belonged. When I had exhausted all the resources I could find about the paranormal, I began to study what paranormal teams were doing out in the field. I studied the photography methods that were being used and later began to listen to audio recordings. It wasn't until I decided to try audio recording for myself that I discovered that I seem to have a talent for recording and hearing voices of the dead.

Luann Joly/A. E. Angel, Founder, Whaling City Ghosts. *Courtesy Crystal Washington, WCG*

Because I lead such a haunted life, the very first audio recordings I ever made were done in my own home. Since then, I haven't stopped. Hundreds of clips of Electronic Voice Phenomena, or EVP, fill more hard drives of more computers than I can count. Some of them are frightening, some of them are sad, but all of them are the voices of the dead. I seem to have some gift, or trait that makes spirits want to speak with me, and as time went on, I decided that in order to help prove the existence of ghosts—life after death—I needed to put together a team with traits similar to mine.

Over the years, I have collected a team of women who have had repeated experiences with the paranormal. I'd like to introduce you to this team of special women I've put together. For with them, I have become just what I always hoped to be—the leader of a team of extraordinary people who, together, make up Whaling City Ghosts.

GABRIELLE LAWSON
CO-FOUNDER/HEAD OF SCHIENTIFIC RESEARCH

Gabrielle Lawson, Co-founder/ Head of Scientific Research.

"Gabby" has wanted to be a chemist since childhood. Even the person she idolized, Madame Curie, showed that she has had an interest in chemistry ever since she could remember. She followed her dreams and attended Regis College of Weston, Massachusetts, and later, did graduate course work at The School of Public Health. For over twenty years, Gabby has worked as an analytical research chemist.

Gabby's love of science has helped to develop the framework of Whaling City Ghosts' approach to investigating the paranormal. In a laboratory setting, conditions can be firmly controlled, but in the paranormal world, there are never any controlled conditions. By using a simplified form of scientific method, we both agree that by logging and recording what we experience in the field, we can try to prove or disprove the existence of ghosts.

Together, Gabby and I have discussed our ideas, exploring possibilities that are infinite. She is one of the most open minded people I know, and because of her, my own ideas have grown. Gabby's warm heart and outgoing personality make her an integral part of this team. Her cool and analytical mind helps her to find new ways to break the barriers that separate the living from the dead. Gabby never stops thinking or trying to learn new things, and in doing so, she has helped to build our team into what it has become today.

RENÉ CARR LEAD INVESTIGATOR

René Carr, Lead Investigator.
Courtesy René Carr

René has always had an interest in the paranormal. She is everything you could ask for in an investigator. Working for over twenty years on the Massachusetts Correctional Force, her experience brings a new element to the field. She doesn't take anything at face value and always looks for causes of possible activity when in the field. René does much of the videography and photography for the team. She enjoys trying new equipment in the field and interacting with spirits in ways that most people wouldn't think of. René might play an authentic Native American drum for the spirits, or purchase an antique toy for a child ghost.

René loves the outdoors and has found a connection with the Wampanoag (Local Native American tribe) spirits in our area and has found places, unknown to many, where the Native American spirits of this country still dwell. She has such a wide variety of interests that her knowledge is valuable and extensive. Working as an "independent" in the field for many years before joining Whaling City Ghosts made her a seasoned investigator who is an asset to any team!

CRYSTAL WASHINGTON LEAD INVESTIGATOR/ WEBSITE DESIGNER/TECH MANAGER/"GADGET GIRL"

Crystal's love of gadgets and the paranormal have made her the kind of investigator every team wishes it had! She has style and true curiosity along with a

Crystal Washington, Lead Investigator/Website Designer/Technical, Manager/"Gadget Girl."
Courtesy Crystal Washington, WCG

sense of humor that keeps the rest of us sane in some difficult circumstances. We never know what to expect, but she makes our lives colorful and I know we couldn't be the team we are without her. Crystal might come into a room with "night-vision goggles" or a "bionic ear," or some other strange device none of us have ever seen before. But she's never afraid to apply her ideas to our investigations. Though she usually tries to hide behind her sense of humor, there is no person I'd rather have at my side when the stuff starts hitting the fan.

Courageous is a word I can use to describe her, and though she wouldn't admit it, she's one of the bravest people I know! "Gadget Girl" also handles much of our photography needs, and I'm sure you'll enjoy her photographs that are included in this book. Crystal also designs the Whaling City Ghosts' website which you will be invited to visit and enjoy, its new special section dedicated to the EVP told about here.

DEBBY WHITE-PAIVA HEAD OF HISTORICAL RESEARCH

If you could carry an encyclopedia of south eastern Massachusetts history, its name would be Debby White-Paiva! Debby

Debby White-Paiva, Head of Historical Research.
Courtesy René Carr

has a passion for research and a strong curiosity for the paranormal which makes her widely sought out for her knowledge and expertise. Many local teams and independent investigators come to Debby when they need historical information, and over the years, she has done research for some big names in the paranormal field. She, eventually, ended up with our sister team, Starborn Support, a group that helps people who have experienced interaction with UFOs or alien abductions. Because of her background in historical research, she was a perfect fit for Whaling City Ghosts.

Debby works relentlessly and brings us information that helps us not only to identify our ghosts, but to understand them. Together, she and I have come up with some new theories on how environmental conditions, like contaminants or geological conditions, such as a high quartz content, can affect a haunting. Between my ideas and her research skills, we hope to come closer to some answers on why New England is such a hotbed of paranormal activity. We are glad that she decided to make Whaling City Ghosts her team!

TARA MONTEMBAULT TEAM PHYCHIC

Tara works as a psychic for a local metaphysical shop in New Bedford, Massachusetts, called III Suns. For a person who started out as another one of my experiments with psychic skills in the paranormal world, she sure has grown on us! Tara has a truly golden heart that can't help from shining. Ghosts I have known and loved for years took to her immediately and began to communicate with her. Because of her experience doing psychic readings, it was a natural step for her to put her skills to use with humans who were no longer a part of the living community. Tara can't hide her heart, even from the dead, and with her, I have found that my audio recordings have become more detailed because of her cues to us as she "reads" the spirits we come into contact with in the field. Tara's excitement in the field gives her a fresh outlook on how she uses her skills. She describes what she does as "putting up a circle" and the spirits who trust her can enter the circle and "show her things." Much of what she gets is visual, but by describing her visions to me, I can then use them to question the spirits more accurately. For years, Whaling City Ghosts ran without a Team Psychic, and after having Tara with us, I don't know how we ever did without her!

Tara Montembault, Team Psychic.
Courtesy Ground Glass Video and
Photography, Brian and Deb Rapoza

So now that you've met my team, you might wonder what drives a person to build a team that would attract more ghosts than we know what to do with. Then again, more than likely, you don't lead a haunted life. I hinted a bit earlier about being haunted myself, but I didn't explain what it means to me to be in the field. Judging by my own research, I am one of thousands upon thousands of people who experience the paranormal regularly. Is it as some people believe, that our souls are "coming through more aware" because of a natural process of evolution? Is it some physical trait that makes this group of people more attractive to the dead somehow?

Is it both of these things? I've tended to go more with the theory of both to answer the questions and that there may also be things that I, as a living human, can not see or understand. Even with my history of paranormal experiences and one of the most extraordinary cases that I have personally ever seen, I have come no closer to answers than anyone else out there.

In the beginning, when I had no other case but my own to judge by, I decided that I would find answers in science, or possibly medicine. I didn't know how close I was to the heart of matters then; but now, I realize that my only choice was, and is, to remain open to possibilities. For even now, I see more doorways opening than I ever dreamed of. My mind keeps wandering back to that phrase, "There are other worlds than these," and I realize that everything I'd touched upon, everything I had experienced, in some inexplicable way, pointed to the truth in these words. I used to look away from Earth, toward space, time itself. But, lately, I realize that there is a strong possibility that many of these worlds I've been looking for may reside right here with us, maybe even under our very feet. Or here beside us, breathing down our necks each and every day.

Maybe my soul did come through more aware, for I even remember a life before this, one that wasn't *this* life, and which confused me as a child. I had no access to information about past lives. I had a very solid scientific upbringing when I grew up. My father was an electrical engineer and my mother had a Ph.D. in Psychology. There were no such things as ghosts, no lives other than this. Facts, science, the amazing human brain were all responsible for these things and they weren't real.

Yet, when I would go to sleep at night, strange things took place. Even during my waking hours, I just might hear my name called, even if no one was there. Taking to the books in my house to search for answers, I knew I wasn't schizophrenic or delusional. I wasn't imagining the things that happened to me; there were too many signs that they were real. But still, there were never any answers, and I hoped that by ignoring everything that happened, the strangeness would just go away. It never did.

It still hasn't. Each and every day, I live in the company of the dead. Even now, I have two female spirits, Emily, a child of about 7 years of age and Rita, a grown woman who, as I've become accustomed to her, I have realized is like a mother figure to me. Recently, I learned just how great the love of these two spirits really was for me.

One of the investigations that you will read about shortly was a difficult case and Whaling City Ghosts had not intended to become involved with it. Sometimes, things beyond our control happen and I found myself living with a dead murderer. Going from a quiet house, where the spirits know "the rules" of my home and are quiet and courteous of the living, to a place where an angry spirit throws objects violently and walks through my room while I am naked, fresh out of the shower, was abrupt. Finding myself not amused with a male presence in my living space, I tried to identify who he could be. But a sinking suspicion that this was not a "good" spirit kept creeping into the back of my mind. It became more evident a few days later.

After hearing something being knocked over in my kitchen, my youngest son, who was visiting at the time, grabbed his cell phone and started taking pictures. Amazingly, he caught the man I'd been seeing wandering my house and peeping at me naked. But what really surprised me was that when I took a good look at the pictures, I noticed that there were what appeared to be females in the picture, too. Even as I tell you this, my heart fills with love for my good friend and spirit, Rita, for I take it as her trying to protect me from this man. Murderer he was in life, violent and angry he is in death. I do not welcome him and I believe that when I ask him to leave, Rita will stand beside me, pointing out the inter-dimensional doorway to him!

Yes, I do believe that the world of spirits exists. I have known no other world since I came to dwell upon this planet, Earth. Though, I search for answers in medicine and in science, I know that many of the answers can be found within our very hearts. We are just small humans, floating amongst the stars, maybe with worlds unseen floating above and below us. We do not have all the answers. But from my own life, my own world, I see that some day maybe these things won't be such mysteries. That maybe as we evolve as a species, we will learn some very special things about ourselves and our souls. Will it, some day, be possible for us to move freely among the other worlds that exist around us? To communicate with beings from other places? To understand that death isn't really an ending, but just a beginning? For me, I like to think so. And I hope that, some day, I will get to travel these worlds. But then again, maybe I already have.

So enter, now, the world of Whaling City Ghosts, where the spirits dwell. Where you call out to the unknown, and the unknown answers back! Enter a world of unlimited possibilities and learn to love our ghosts just as much as we do. Once upon a time, each of the ghosts described in this book was just as alive as you and I are now. Maybe, someday, *we* will be the ghosts and they will be among the living who question us. But I do know that if you listen to the voices of the dead—their whispers—you just might learn something about yourself that you never knew. And I invite you to learn, to think, to grow, and to evolve. For as we grow, so too does science. Right now, none of us have the answers to the great questions, but if we break the barriers of what we know today, we will have the answers of tomorrow!

So come in, if you dare; I think you'll enjoy your stay with us. Meet the ghosts of New England that have made our lives special and who, in their own way, have lessons to teach us. For if they can still be here after all the centuries, if they can touch us across all those worlds, then maybe they have more for us than we can ever know!

A WORD ABOUT
ELECTRONIC VOICE PHENOMENON

"The Gathering."
Courtesy Crystal Washington, WCG

One of my greatest passions is recording the voices of the dead and I hope to share it with you. Electronic Voice Phenomenon, or EVP, is a learned skill. The more you practice with it, the better you get. As I prepared the EVP for this book, I worked with many living people to come up with the best way to present them to those who may never have listened to EVP before.

The reason that these recorded voices of the dead are called "Electronic Voice Phenomenon" is simply because we are using an electronic devise to record auditory sounds that are not in the normal range of human hearing. Though, on some occasions, we are lucky enough to catch sounds audibly, called Auditory Voice Phenomenon, or AVP, most of the time, the responses we get are unheard by our frail human ears. By using digital voice recorders, whole new dimensions open up that we would hear no other way.

Now, I do have to admit that some are better at hearing EVP than others. Many think that having a "connection" to the other side helps. I do not know if this is true or not, but I do show skill with hearing ghost voices; and, over the years, by listening to so many recordings, I believe I have developed this skill. I have a long history with the paranormal, and, from time to time, I would play some of my recordings for friends. I noticed that most of them would shake their heads, not able to hear what I so clearly heard. It made me want to find a way to help them hear these voices from the other side.

Fiddling with the way I presented them, I devised a way of cutting them which I thought would make them more clear for others. What I have done for you here is the same method that I've used to help my friends to hear these clips as clearly as I could. Firstly, my clips are a bit shorter in length than most investigators' clips.

I decided that listening to a bunch of human voices, rather than focusing on the ghost voice was counter productive to what I was trying to do. Most times, unless the human voice is asking a pertinent question, or has some bearing on the EVP itself, I try to keep them out, so as not to confuse the listener. Secondly, I provide a "loop" of the EVP which repeats the phrase three times. Most times, if the listener can not hear the EVP in the original clip, they can hear it in the loop. One of my friends, who is also a client of Whaling City Ghosts, is hard of hearing. He was one of my test subjects. Even he, on hearing the "loop" version of the EVP, could go back and hear it in the original. I suggest that if you have any trouble hearing the EVP included with this book, listen to the loop several times, if necessary; then go back to the original once you can clearly hear it in the loop. This usually helps you to hear the EVP in the original clip.

Do remember that practice makes perfect, so if you have trouble with some, come back to them, listen again. You'll be surprised how the voices seem to "jump out" at you once you've begun to understand them. The more you listen and become accustomed to hearing frequencies that your ears are not precisely attuned to, the more you'll hear. I even find that, at times, when I listen to a clip that I've heard before, things often come out that I didn't hear initially. So take your time and be patient with yourself. These are not sounds we are used to hearing. It's a learned art.

Another thing to remember is that EVP is not an exact science. We use other equipment such as video recorders, digital cameras, electromagnetic field (EMF) detectors, digital thermometers, and other equipment to help us determine if ghosts are present. Even using such equipment, it has not been proven that any of these devices can truly detect the presence of spirits. Using video cameras with infrared vision that can see in the dark can capture human shapes on film, but many times, the video is not reviewed until a later date. Many believe that when ghosts manifest, they produce an electromagnetic field that can be detected using an EMF detector. As of yet, we have no proof that this is actually true, we can only record the data and hope that it matches up frequently enough to say without a doubt that this is true. A digital thermometer can also be useful to record "cold spots" in which a spirit is said to be trying to manifest and is using the available energy in the air, and, in theory, making it colder. It is said that spirits can also make it warmer, by charging the atoms that make up the air in their attempt to draw energy from it. I have experienced both hot and cold spots, and though I do think that this might be the indication of spirits, I do not have enough evidence to prove it.

I promise that I'll keep recording our findings at each investigation and that many others out there will be doing the same; and maybe, some day, I'll be able to say for certain if it somehow relates to the manifestation of spirits.

Using many different types of equipment and by trying new things in the field, we hope to learn more about what exactly a ghost is. Logging our readings and reviewing our evidence can help us to correlate all of the data into a bigger picture. For instance, if I record EVP at the same moment that there was an EMF reading and a huge temperature difference, and it happens repeatedly, we can assume that EMF is related to spirits—that elevations or drops in temperature have something to do with ghosts. But it takes a lot of recording and a lot of data to make these assumptions. In the field, it seems as if nothing is very consistent, but at the same time, we can not have a controlled atmosphere, as we can in laboratory settings.

Maybe the future will bring a way to enclose the location of a haunt. To control the atmosphere in a laboratory-like setting. Until then, all we can do is record and log, log and record. I hope that the future brings us more answers. Or maybe we're not meant to ever know all of the secrets that the other side holds. For now, I can only keep reaching out into the unknown, calling out to it, with the hope that it continues to reach back out to me. That I will always hear its call. For, to me, the paranormal has become a way of life. I hope that with each step I take into the unknown, I can take all of you with me. That you learn to believe in the human soul, and to believe in yourself. For I do believe that somehow there is deeper meaning to this, something that we can't see. But no matter the meaning, for each of us to learn and to grow, to become what we are destined to be, we each must take that first step.

For those of you who take that first step, I hope it is a journey you will continue to pursue. I really do believe that if we listen to the voices and the history of our pasts we can make our futures that much brighter. I can not view this journey we call life as living, working, dying. I see it as a beginning and then another beginning. For, to me, life is a circle, with no beginning, no ending. I think after we leave this world behind, we really do go on. The voices of the dead have a message to pass on, so listen carefully, and maybe you will hear it, too!

HOW TO INTERPRET THE AUDIO FILES

Each audio file is listed with a file name and number according to which chapter of the book its story is located and where it falls within the chapter. Every file has the original EVP at the beginning, then a moment of silence. A loop file follows, which repeats the EVP three times and concludes each file. Listen as many times as you like. Remember, the more you listen, the more you'll hear.

Now, I do admit I have good sound equipment, audio programs, and a good set of headphones, but I have tried to provide you with audio clips that can be heard easily. If you are still having trouble hearing the clips, it might be because of your sound equipment. If this is the case, you could try a public system, such as the library, or a friend or family member's equipment. Listening in a quiet atmosphere, where you can be relaxed and at your ease can be conducive to a good audio session. Also remember that too much of a good thing can be bad—even I never listen to audio for long periods of time. If I am distracted or stressed, I never do audio work. So consider your demeanor going into any audio session for best results.

Though I feel the following EVP classes are for more experienced listeners, it is still important information to know, especially if you plan to learn more about the paranormal.

See the class definitions below:

- **Class A EVPs:** easily heard and understood by everyone
- **Class B EVPS:** not as easily understood and some will not be able to recognize the words
- **Class C EVPs:** not heard or understood readily, and most will not be able to make out the words being said.

I have tried to furnish you with mainly Class A EVPs for the *Dead Whispers* audio CD. With practice, you should be able to hear and understand all of the clips provided.

If you remember my tips as you listen, you should have a great experience hearing the *dead whispers* that ring through into our world. I hope it is an experience you never forget, and that the spirits I've met change your life, just as they have mine. For me, knowing that there is life after life fills me with hope. I can't help but wonder what adventures I will meet when I leave this world. Where I will go and what I will become are questions I can not answer, but I do know that I will go on. And so will you!

AUTHOR NOTE

This is a quick sample view of how you will see the book's EVPs, along with their formatting that corresponds to the actual recordings on the enclosed CD as noted earlier.

The following example shows the Track Number, followed by a line that displays the chapter number, and quick word explanation of what you will be hearing.

RECORDING

Track 2
[1 Can't Change Life I Can't Change]

The sample shows that Track 2 is an EVP discussed in Chapter 1, placed as the first EVP in the chapter, and the words you will be striving to hear, "Can't change life; I can't change."

Note that Track 1 on the CD is an Introduction and that the EVPs begin with Track 2.

Remember that it takes time and practice to hear some of the Class B and C EVPs, whereas Class A material is quite clear.

Practice, practice, practice!

CHAPTER ONE

THE QUEQUECHAN CLUB

A GENTLEMAN'S CLUB WITH SPIRIT

The Victorian era, which began in 1837 and ended in 1901, was also known as the "Gilded Age." Members of high society built bigger, more elaborate homes, feasted on French cuisine made by French chefs they imported from France, and threw gigantic parties. Families from "old money" were generally accepted in society, while "new money" was usually only accepted if they were extremely wealthy, or had married into an old money family. Male members of the high society of Fall River, Massachusetts decided to begin a gentleman's club and started out by purchasing a mansion on Main Street that was known as the William Mason Estate. By December of 1894, the Quequechan (koe-ka-shan) Club was incorporated. In 1919, the club bought the Dr. Hubert Wilbur home next door, which later became known as "The Priscilla Room" to function as a ladies' annex. Today, the building still holds the antique furnishings, bowling alley, and pool tables that once graced it during its days as a club where the gentleman of wealth could enjoy all the finer things in life. I have reason to believe some of these gentleman still wander the halls and banquet rooms of the Quequechan Club.

The word "quequechan" loosely translated means "falling river" in the Wampanoag (local Native American tribe that was decimated during "King Philip's War")

From the outside, the Quequechan Club looks like any other historic building in the area. You'd never suspect so many ghosts lurk inside. *Courtesy Eric LaVoie, DART Paranormal* language, as the building rests on the east bank of what is presently known as the Taunton River. The Quequechan River once emptied itself into the Taunton River, but now runs underground next to the highway that cuts through the center of Fall River.

Looking out the back windows of the building affords a breathtaking view of the Charles M. Braga Memorial Bridge. Battleship Cove can be seen just below the bridge. These modern-day sites seem out of place when one is on the inside of the building where most of the original antiques have been lovingly cared for. Furnishings and accoutrements have been so well preserved that you feel as if you've stepped inside a time machine and come out on the other side into the Victorian era. I have to wonder, if this were possible, what would I see if I entered the Quequechan Club? Would I find the gentleman bowling, playing pool, smoking cigars and pipes, seated in leather chairs set in front of sumptuous fireplaces? Would there be ladies at their sides? Ladies who weren't their lawfully wedded spouses?

I can't help but wonder, for their wives weren't allowed in the club, not even to dine with their husbands. To enter and exit the building, to use facilities they were allowed to use, the ladies were forced to walk through a coal cellar. It wasn't until the middle of the 1970s, when the women became frustrated with these rules and stormed the club, that they were finally allowed to enter.

You see, there is a rumor that the third floor of the building housed a brothel, and I speculate if this is the reason why the men were so adamant that their wives remain excluded from most of the amenities the club boasted. I can't help but question if a spirit named Marie was truly a lady of the night in this brothel...or ponder if she was forced into a life of prostitution.

Quality prostitutes were usually acquired, either through a powerful madame or purveyors of human slaves. Many don't realize that human slavery didn't end with the Civil War, and that it even goes on today. In my mind's eye, I can imagine Marie, poor, threadbare, but clean, clothes, beautiful, with flashing dark eyes. She walks through a Victorian-era city, hoping to find work, maybe in a mill or stitching away in a sweat shop. I feel her fear as they creep up behind her, pulling a sackcloth bag over her head and whisking her away. I have no way of knowing if this is true, but I do know that Marie still wanders the rooms of the Quequechan Club. I also know she isn't alone.

OFFICIAL INVESTIGATION
AUGUST 29, 2009

Eric LaVoie of DART (Dartmouth Anomalies Research Team) invited me to join him to investigate the Quequechan Club with hopes that the female spirits in the suspected brothel area on the third floor would bond with me. Joining us that night were Tim Weisberg, Matt Costa, and Matt Moniz, better known as the "Spooky

Crew," as they operate our local haunted radio show *Spooky Southcoast*. Also with us were Andrew Lake of Greenville Paranormal and Mike Marcowicz ("The EVP Man"). Eric had been here before and felt there might be some truth to the brothel rumor, for he had recorded female spirits that seemed to be in turmoil. He thought that having a female investigator on scene would help the spirits of possible prostitutes to communicate more freely. He was right!

Tropical Storm Danny was passing by this night and weather conditions were pretty wild. Many believe that certain changes in weather and atmospheric conditions can help spirit activity to manifest. Humidity was at 100 percent, winds were gusting, occasional thunder would rumble overhead, and rain periodically spattered down.

Inside the building, conditions were much more comfortable. I couldn't help but admire the furnishings and antiques that graced the large, tastefully appointed rooms. The atmosphere was welcoming, and I felt immediately at home. I couldn't wait to meet the "girls" on the third floor.

As if he'd read my mind, Eric LaVoie showed us the way to the third floor, where the alleged brothel was said to have existed at one time. After climbing the winding staircases, we found ourselves in an area much different from the lower levels of the building. Construction and restoration were in progress here. One large room with smaller rooms attached around it was unfinished. Tools and ladders were placed around the edges, leaving us just enough room to set up our equipment and settle in for an EVP session.

Not long before this investigation, Eric LaVoie had donated a "Hack Shack" to Whaling City Ghosts because he knew I was interested in experimenting with one. I decided I'd try it out here to see if any of the spirits would be willing to communicate with us through the device. A Hack Shack is an inexpensive AM/FM radio (originally purchased from Radio Shack) that has had the "seek" pin removed, so that once you begin scanning through the channels, it cannot stop on any frequency and it continues to scan through all the channels. The theory is that the spirits can use the frequencies to communicate with us. I hadn't had a chance to use it yet and thought it might be helpful. I had added a splitter to the device so that I could listen with headphones, while recording it simultaneously. As soon as I placed the headphones on my ears, I began to hear the name "Marie" and the words "whore" and "rape." I blurted out the phrases I could hear in hopes that it would give the other investigators a line of questioning for the traditional recorders we were all running.

Pulling the headphones from my head, I related what I'd heard to the others. While I was speaking to them, a sweet and sing-song EVP voice pipes in, at times, over my voice. I know I was the only female present in the building that night; therefore, I find I can't help but wonder if this was Marie.

"Can't change life, I can't change," always brings sadness to my heart when I hear it.

Track 2
[1 Can't Change Life I Can't Change]

RECORDING

I find myself thinking about the real story behind "Marie," whether she'd been kidnapped and forced into prostitution, and, so in her mind, "raped." I can only guess at what she meant by these words; I can only feel her sadness. When I listen to her sweet voice, I realize that though she didn't enjoy the life she was forced to lead, she felt as if there was nothing she could do about it, and so accepted what life handed her. As sweet and sad as she sounds, I find myself admiring her courage and bravery when faced with circumstances I can't imagine being stuck in.

Spooky Southcoast broadcast a live show from the Quequechan Club that night from a room on the second floor. Much as I enjoy listening to the show, I felt pulled to return to the third floor. Leaving the men behind, I crept up the stairs to the brothel area, set up my Hack Shack and digital recorders, sat down, and hoped I could coax the spirits to tell me more. Placing the headphones back on my head, I listened to the stream of words as they flew by. I was sure I heard the name "Preston" quite a few times, along with the name "Marie," repeated over and over again.

23

The Hack Shack can be quite brutal on your ears, as the channels tick by constantly and blurbs of words and sounds assault your ear drums. I placed the headphones down next to one of my recorders and started questioning the spirits I suspected were present. All alone on the third floor, I swore that I felt a male presence with me. It wasn't until later, on evidence review, that I learned I was right.

During my stay in the brothel area, I kept feeling as if my hair was catching on something. Knowing how high the humidity was that night, I passed it off as a bad-hair day. Humidity makes my hair frizzy and I kept thinking to myself that this was all it was—humidity and frizzy hair go together. Later, after watching Eric LaVoie's video capture of an orb flying around the room in a strange pattern, then swooping by my head seeming to pop my ponytail to the side, made me think it might be more than just a bad-hair day—it could be something else.

Moments before this video capture, the Hack Shack blurts out something that, to this day, is still a mystery. *"Have the book, I'm F'ing dead,"* has a distinct accent to it.

RECORDING **Track 3**
[1 Have The Book Im Fing Dead]

It sounds rather Irish, possibly Scottish, and I asked myself: *Just what book is he talking about?*

Hearing this unmistakable male voice coming through the Hack Shack illustrated that this piece of equipment was a very useful tool. I find it highly unlikely that the same voice with the same accent could cover so many stations as they flashed by. Each tick, and the music that filters through at one point, is a separate radio station.

Most of the original furnishings are still in residence in the Quequechan Club, including the grandfather clock which was donated to the club in 1895. *Courtesy Eric LaVoie, DART Paranormal*

I also knew using language such as I'd heard with this EVP on the radio would get that broadcasting station one heck of an FCC fine. I decided I'd have to experiment more with this handy device.

Shortly after, another strange Hack Shack hit came through the headphones and onto my digital recorder. This recording showed me that these particular spirits are aware; they are spirits who *want* my attention.

"Hey Luann!" sounds like more than one female calling my name.

 **Track 4**
[1 Hey Luann]

I admit that you may hear my name on the radio if you're listening to *Spooky Southcoast;* but other than that, I can't say I've heard my name anywhere else. With all the members of the Spooky Crew being male and serious researchers, I do not believe that it was them singing my name on their radio show.

After reviewing the rest of the recordings from that night, I realized the spirits wanted Marie to communicate with me. I considered whether they hoped I could help her in some way; she seemed so fragile to me, and the other spirits seemed to want to protect her. It only piqued my curiosity more to hear a female telling Marie to speak to me. (This EVP not included.)

Placing the headphones back on my head, I listened to words as they flashed by and I swore that I again heard the name "Princeton" or "Preston" repeatedly. The stations and words go by so quickly, it's hard to pick up on everything that is said. Not really sure if I had the correct name, I asked the empty room, "Did you come here and visit the girls here, Preston?" After a pause, a small voice answers, *"Maybe a little bit."*

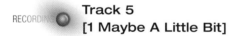 **Track 5**
[1 Maybe A Little Bit]

When I heard this during evidence review, I couldn't help but smile; it's always nice to know an honest ghost!

After evidence review for this case, I was convinced that a spirit named Marie did indeed exist. I couldn't understand how this fragile woman had ended up there and who the other spirits that seemed so protective of her really were. I speculated whether Preston had been in love with her, and what exactly the mysterious book was. I hadn't asked about a book, but it had to be important to at least one of the ghosts still in residence at the Quequechan Club. I could only hope to be able to return again and ask; I could only hope I'd get an answer.

For a club that hadn't allowed women to enter I had felt right at home, encouraged by the spirits to learn more about them. A strange bond seemed to have formed between myself and the ghosts of the Quequechan Club and I felt as if they wanted to tell me their stories. Over the last few years, I've often longed to return and get to know them better. Recently, my wish came true.

OFFICIAL INVESTIGATION
FEBRUARY 11, 2012

Once again, Eric LaVoie of DART contacted me about the Quequechan Club. I was more than happy to help him film an episode of the television show, *My Ghost Story.* I was also excited to re-enter the Quequechan Club, in hopes of learning more about Marie and the mysterious book. I hopped into the back of Eric's SUV for the trip to Fall River, Massachusetts. Enjoying ghostly conversation with Eric and Paul Hebard, Jr., his teammate, made the trip go quickly.

During the short drive to the Quequechan Club, I related to Eric that I was interested in knowing if anyone had found any old books in the building, telling him of the Hack Shack hit I'd made during our prior investigation. Immediately, Eric asked me to repeat what the EVP said. I did my best to imitate the voice I'd heard, "Have the book, I'm F'ing dead," I told him in a terrible Irish accent. Eric related to me that the owner of the building, Dan Silva, had found an old book that related the history and transactions of the club from the day it was opened. I was amazed and hoped that this was the book the spirit spoke of.

We began by setting up a camera on the third floor in the same area it had been placed when Eric caught the strange orb activity that set my ponytail to motion. Since Eric and the owner, Dan, were needed by the film man, Paul and I paired off and explored the building, trying to stay out of their way. Though we explored all the rooms in the building, marveling at the care in which the antiques and furnishings had been kept, we found we couldn't stay away from the third floor. We felt as if we were being followed; a shadow kept popping up, just in our peripheral vision. Each time, we'd follow after it, hoping to see either what had caused it, or to catch it in action. No matter how many times we chased down the mysterious shadow, we were unsuccessful in finding a cause, or an apparition. We both felt as if something was playing with us, teasing us in its own way. Maybe it was trying to lead us to the book?

Eric joined us on the third floor while Dan was interviewed. As we stood discussing some of DART's new equipment, my cell phone rang. My younger son was calling, so I answered, in hopes that it wouldn't be an emergency. After relaying the fact that I would be unavailable for the night, I proceeded in shutting the phone down, so we wouldn't be disturbed by more phone calls and to cut down on any EMF or random signals that could corrupt our evidence.

"I'll be seeing you," is whispered by a male voice just before I say, in my "high society" accent, "Luann isn't taking calls right now."

 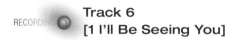
Track 6
[1 I'll Be Seeing You]

I'm not sure if this is in response to telling my son, "Goodbye," at the end of our conversation. Maybe, he thought I was leaving, or possibly he knows something I don't—that I'll be back in the building in the future. (I can only hope so, for the ghosts in the Quequechan Club make me more curious about them every time I visit!)

The film man had asked that Eric set up his equipment the way he had it the night he captured the strange orb that flicked my ponytail, so we all went downstairs to get the rest of the boxes and cases he had brought with him.

In the recording, you can hear us *clomping* down the stairs, and my voice in the distance. Closer to the recorder a voice utters the word, *"Farming."*

Track 7
[1 Farming]

The strange accent gave me the idea that he might be a southern plantation owner who came to access the facilities and pleasures that the Quequechan Club had to offer. I do think I heard from this spirit again, but that came later, after more clues about the mysterious book.

Ornate woodwork graces most of the rooms and this small tavern on the first floor is no exception. *Courtesy Eric LaVoie, DART Paranormal*

Paul and I decided to do some EVP work upstairs while Eric was busy interviewing for the TV show. What better place to do it than on the third floor, where the alleged brothel had been? Since I knew that the spirit named Marie seemed to be a key player in this haunt, I kept calling her name and asking if she was there.

In the next clip, you can hear my voice calling for Marie, and then two EVPs follow. *"The book is ripped... The book is with Marie,"* sounds as if it is possibly two separate spirits speaking of the book.

RECORDING 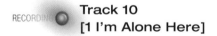 **Track 8**
[1 The Book is Ripped Book Is With Marie]

The fact that the spirits keep mentioning this book makes me wonder if owner Dan Silva, really did find the book the spirits were referencing. Could there be another book in the building that hasn't been found? The size of the building makes it impossible to say if there is some hidden place that hasn't been discovered. The basement is finished and houses a bowling alley, tavern, and pool tables, while the first and second floors have spacious rooms and banquet halls. The third floor has finished rooms with windows overlooking the river, along with the unfinished rooms that are suspected to be the brothel area. One of the unfinished rooms still holds various boxes and crates. Could the book be hidden among them?

Shortly after this EVP, Paul and I join Eric and the film man downstairs.

As we walk away from the recorders, two more EVPs pipe in. The first is a strange laugh.

RECORDING **Track 9**
[1 Laugh]

Since I can't hear what we're talking about, I can't say if this spirit is laughing at something we've said, or if he's laughing at us.

The second clip reminds me of the voice from a previous EVP, "Farming." It seems to have a somewhat southern accent. *"I'm alone here,"* comes shortly after the laugh.

RECORDING **Track 10**
[1 I'm Alone Here]

I found myself wondering if he was lonely, since we had left him behind on the third floor. He must prefer the company of the living, since it seems to me he's got plenty of ghostly friends for companionship.

28

Eric joined us on the third floor while the film man was busy interviewing Dan. Though the rest of the building is much more comfortable and elegant, you can't spend time in this building and not feel pulled to visit the third floor. Soon, we were all pulled away from the brothel area by Dan, who had prepared a feast for us downstairs. I didn't know that I had recorded a full name while on the third floor, but as soon as I reached the first floor and sat down, I found myself needing to wander to a small alcove close to the front entrance of the building.

Up against one wall, an antique table stood, and above it, certificates with names on them hung from the wall. For some reason, I needed to write down the names on the certificate on the left. I moved to my equipment bag, grabbed a pen and pad of paper and copied the name, John Murroe, from the certificate. The certificate announced that John Murroe was the billiards champion for the year 1897-1898. It was signed by F.O. Dodge, who was the original purchaser of the building in 1894, and E.L. Hawkins.

Little did I know that John Murroe had made his presence known upstairs in the brothel area. *"John Murroe,"* comes toward the end of this recording as a whisper, but it is quite clear that John wanted to introduce himself to us.

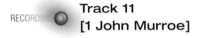

RECORDING

Track 11
[1 John Murroe]

Later, I set Debby White-Paiva on the name and she found something strange. In Fall River, Massachusetts, there is a "John Murroe" and a "John Munroe" listed. They both have the same birthday, and she wonders if John Murroe had changed his name to Munroe to seem more American. John Munroe is listed as the owner of the *Fall River Daily Herald* and published several books, including *Dillon's Catholic Directory of Fall River.* Are John Murroe and John Munroe one and the same? Is the directory he wrote the book the spirits speak about? I can only hope that more time will help us to solve this 114-year old mystery.

Sitting down, we gathered in the first-floor tavern to enjoy the feast Dan had prepared for us. He had fresh rolls to put chourico and peppers in, wonderful little egg rolls and Philly steak and cheese rolls, grapes, and crackers were set on a plate close by. Dan always makes us feel right at home, and I have to say, he's one heck of a cook!

As we enjoyed the rare ghost hunters' feast, a strange EVP filters in around our conversation. *"Rare meat, I don't like it,"* seems to express distaste for what we were being served.

RECORDING

Track 12
[1 Rare Meat I Don't Like It]

Chourico is a Portuguese sausage with a bit of spice to it, and the Philly steak rolls were cooked to perfection. Since chourico is a red-colored sausage, it is possible the ghost thought it wasn't cooked properly. Either that, or we had a vegetarian ghost in the room with us.

The last EVP for the night was taken on the first floor. We were discussing a door upstairs that we thought had possibly been moved, for Paul and I had heard a strange creaking sound earlier and hadn't been able to find an explanation for it. We did find a door that was ajar, and when we moved it, the sound was very similar to the one we'd heard.

Paul's voice is very strong in the beginning of this clip, telling us to, "Lock the door," while my voice is a bit softer. Between his voice and mine, a spirit asks, "What you want," then a slightly different voice says, "Hello." (Not included.)

Not long after, we began breaking down equipment and packing everything up for the ride home. As we were driving away, I couldn't help but look back at the beautiful building and consider whether I'd ever get to visit these interesting spirits again...if I'd ever learn the mystery of the "book."

CONCLUDING QUEQUECHAN CLUB

Investigating the Quequechan Club was a rare treat that I hope to revisit in the future. Not only is the building itself beautiful and well kept, but the spirits are aware and charming. During our last investigation, Eric LaVoie captured an apparition that appears in the hallway before the camera. This footage can be seen on the DART website (see Resource page at the end of this book), so you can visit his team's site and judge for yourself. I can tell you that Paul and I experienced this many times during the night, chasing down phantoms that we were too slow to catch. I can only wonder if the spirit Eric caught on film was the same one we'd chased without luck all night long.

What I do know about the Quequechan Club only makes me want to know more about this elegant gentleman's establishment and the spirits who remain behind, haunting its luxurious hallways. Did a brothel really exist on the third floor? Who is Marie? Why do all the spirits seem so concerned about her? What is this mysterious book?

Looking to the future I hope, at some point, to gain Marie's trust, along with the other spirits here and to find out the answers to my questions. Someday, I want to turn the pages of *the book*, and learn why it is so important to people who have

Tasteful décor surrounds an original marble fireplace on the second floor.
Courtesy Eric LaVoie, DART Paranormal

been dead for many years, but still inhabit a place that must have been very special to them. At this time, I don't have all the answers, but I hope that with more research, more investigation, and more contact with the wonderful spirits of the Quequechan Club, I will get closer to knowing the truth that hides behind the mystery.

I feel a bond with these ghosts, and I hope the feeling is mutual, that with time, I will know them all, the history they lived, the love they felt, and how they died. Most of all, I'd like to know why they still roam the rooms here, protecting a shy, seemingly vulnerable spirit named Marie. I hope that somehow, some way, they all find peace on the other side.

The Quequechan Club is a private club, protected by a high-tech security system. Please respect the owner and the spirits who dwell there. Only members of the club are allowed to enter and access the facilities of the building. Eric LaVoie and Dan Silva are close friends and I assure you, DART is the only team that will be allowed on the premises. Please do not contact Dan or the Quequechan Club to enter or investigate. I'd like to follow the wishes of the club and its owner, so please do help protect this wonderful haunt.

TIP

The number one rule of safe ghost hunting is to never trespass. Always seek permission to visit private sites. Many public locations are happy to work with teams and ghost enthusiasts and offer special passes for nighttime visits. Call ahead and find out before entering any location. Happy hunting!

CHAPTER TWO

SALEM, MASSACHUSETTS

MORE THAN JUST THE WITCH CITY

CITY OF WITCHES, SEPTEMBER 2008

Salem, Massachusetts is known for the witch trials that went on in 1692, but there is a rich history here that most people don't even know about. The witch trials are just a small part of what Salem was, and has, become. Fishing, farming, and sea trade were all important parts of this beautiful city. They have embraced their rich history and made it one of the most wonderful places to visit! As the mayor of Salem explained to us, this is a great walking city, where everything is close by and tourists are encouraged to get out and explore the streets. Many of the businesses cater to the witch history, and the witch logo can be found everywhere—even on the police cars. The sidewalks are loaded with vendors and I found the city not only friendly, but absolutely charming!

Whaling City Ghosts' trip included some friends. Robb Kaczor of Other Side Paranormal Investigations (OSPI) from Michigan came along with some good friends of his from *Allure Media Productions*, in Texas, Greg Sitler and John Beuche. Robb was a seasoned investigator that Whaling City Ghosts had worked with many times; Greg and John were skeptics who weren't sure if they believed in ghosts. All in all, I think we picked the best city to show them the world of paranormal investigation. Not only was Salem beautiful and rich with history, it was a very haunted city!

We all stayed at the Salem Inn, which, at the time, had never been investigated. We found our rooms very comfortable and quaint. The rooms we had boasted jacuzzis. Unfortunately, I never found time to enjoy it, but my son, Tyler, just over surgery on his arm, enjoyed it at will. Because of the cast on his arm, and our busy schedule about town, he was the first to witness one of the spirits that reside at the Salem Inn. (More about that later!)

The Salem Inn was actually comprised of three buildings at different locations. We were lucky enough to stay at the largest of them, the Captain Nathaniel West House, which was built in 1834. With approximately twenty-three guest rooms, I found it hard to imagine just one family living there. It was a large brick building, built in the Federal style. As you entered the front door, the hotel desk was directly in front of you, with a common room to the left. In the common room, a lively cage full of finches catches your eye. A glass decanter filled with port wine rests next to a book for guests to sign and tell of their stays at the hotel. As I flipped through the pages of the book, I discovered that some of the guests had experienced ghostly happenings.

Most of the accounts I read did not seem threatening in any way. It seemed more as if the spirits simply wanted to make contact. I was intrigued and could hardly wait to begin investigating this beautiful building. We spent the first day exploring the city and doing many of the tours that run. We met with Joel, who runs a bike tour through the city. He was an amazing wellspring of information and seemed to hold the witch trials close in his heart. He showed respect for those people who were not witches, and would not admit to being witches, even if it meant saving their lives. He pointed out the stones that are the only memorials to the people who once faced death rather than plead guilty to witchcraft. The victims of this horrible atrocity could not be buried in the Christian cemeteries. Instead, their bodies were taken by family members and buried in secret locations. Nineteen of the accused were hung, while Giles Corey was pressed to death. This was done by placing wooden boards over the person's body and putting stones on top of the boards until the job was done. As two days of this torture went by, they repeatedly asked Giles to plead either innocent or guilty to witchcraft. Each time Giles replied only, "More weight." During this process, Giles never cried out as they added more stones to his boards. Witches or not, the accused showed bravery that we only read about today. I, for one, do not think I could have withstood Giles' fate.

As Joel spoke to us, he pointed to the words engraved into the stones that people walked upon as they strolled around the memorial. The stones sat by the burial ground where these victims could never be buried. Words such as: "I am no witch. I am innocent. I know nothing of it," and, "If it was the last moment I was to live, God knows I am innocent..." I'm sure if you have a chance to visit Salem, and read these words for yourself, a chill will run down your spine. Just as it did mine.

Wandering around Salem and enjoying the sights and tours of the city is a hungry business. Before heading back to the Salem Inn to begin the night's investigation, we stopped at Rockafellas Restaurant for dinner. Not only did we enjoy the food and wonderful atmosphere of the building, we got to hear about some of the history. We learned of the infamous "Lady in Blue" ghost who is very possessive of the building. (If you visit not because of the ghosts or the history of the building, then go for the food.) We all enjoyed dinner very much, even though we kept our eyes sharp, just in case the "Lady in Blue" decided to make her presence known. Staring up at the painting of her and the band on the wall, it's easy to speculate what the real story might be, or find yourself thinking about the long history of the building itself. Add in that the underground tunnel used to sneak jewels and precious metals in for the jewelry store that once inhabited the first floor, and you just might find yourself in a true New England ghost story!

Rockafellas now resides in a building that was originally built in 1826 by members of Salem's First Church. The church used the second floor as a place of worship while renting out the first floor to various businesses in order to help pay for the building and maintenance. The building is still named for Daniel Low, who started a jewelry shop in a corner room on the first floor, but soon took over the entire floor. The jewelry business flourished, partly because of a "Witch Spoon" that his company made available all over the country through mail-order catalogs. It remained a family-run business into the 1950s. Daniel Low's son, Seth, ran the business until 1911, with his widow running it until the mid '50s. As mentioned earlier, it is said that the underground tunnels, which exist today, were made by the jewelry store owners to bring in gems and other valuable materials needed to manufacture the jewelry and items they sold. It wasn't until the next day, when we came in to investigate this building, with its long past, that we learned of the whole story behind the legend of the "Lady in Blue."

SALEM INN
OFFICIAL INVESTIGATION
NIGHT ONE

After enjoying a wonderful dinner at Rockafellas Restaurant, we returned to the Salem Inn. Setting up our equipment, we were eager to begin the investigation. I took a small break to check in on my son, and as I visited with him, he explained to me that he had seen a ghost while we were away. He'd been watching television and resting and had gotten bored. (As mentioned, he had recently had surgery on a broken arm.) He decided to explore the hotel a bit, and as he was walking down the hallway on our floor, he saw the spirit of a woman.

His description of her confused me, and the thought crossed my mind that he might be making it all up. He told me it was "sort of weird" for she "walked like an old woman" but "her hair was dark, not gray." He described how she walked with a pantomime of her actions by hunching his shoulders forward and shuffling along with short steps. I listened to his information as my team arrived in my room to prepare for the night's investigation.

Deciding that I would freshen up a bit and brush my teeth, I gathered my toiletries and closed myself into the bathroom. Brushing my hair, I turned the water on to brush my teeth. As I stood there scrubbing my teeth, I felt a pressure on my left shoulder blade area. It felt tingly, and as I looked into the mirror to see if there was

Gabrielle Lawson bringing a boom microphone into The Salem Inn for our investigation. We affectionately named this microphone the "tribble!"
Courtesy Crystal Washington, WCG

anything visual going on, I called out softly to the girls that something was touching me. I was afraid to scare whatever it was away, so I tried not to raise my voice. The pressure on my shoulder remained constant and continued to tingle as I called out to my co-investigators for equipment to take temperature and EMF readings. None of them could hear me, as they were talking and laughing with my son. Finally, I tried calling out more loudly that something was touching me and they came running. Unfortunately, when I yelled out, I seemed to scare away the spirit, for the sensation disappeared. Even so, I couldn't help but wonder if it was the same spirit my son had claimed to see that day.

From the accounts of ghostly occurrences written in the lobby guest book, we could tell that the most active rooms in the building were Rooms 14 and 17. We were lucky enough to be occupying those very rooms and set up video cameras and audio recorders in both of them. Robb set up our Control Room in Room 14, which happened to be the room he was staying in. After running our EMF sweep throughout the hotel rooms and hallway, we decided that we'd cover Room 17, Greg's room, while Robb covered Room 14 with our skeptical friends from Texas, John and Greg.

Our first night of investigation at the Salem Inn seemed to be a bit slow. Gabby, Crystal, and I remained in Room 17 for most of the night. It wasn't until later, after reviewing the audio, that we realized we hadn't been alone that night. Almost immediately after I started my recorder up, I received a greeting from beyond.

A ghostly voice calls out, *"Hello,"* as we move about the room taking EMF readings.

RECORDING **Track 13**
[2 Hello]

Not hearing the voice audibly, we moved about our business, oblivious to the unseen world that had opened up around us. Nothing like a pajama party with paranormal investigators in a historic, haunted hotel in Salem, Massachusetts!

Room 17 seemed peaceful; we continued running EMF and temperature readings, as we tried to settle comfortably about the room to begin an EVP session. Not having much to go on, we used the information that we *did* know about the building to promote responses. Remembering my son's experience earlier that day, and my own in the bathroom, I tried to pose questions to a woman with pain and disability. We tried to cater to the original builder of the house, sea captain Nathaniel West, and any relatives that might be roaming the halls. We all kept checking the meters and snapping shots off as the night went on, but there was no physical manifestation of spirits that we could take note of.

Little did we know that a male voice seemed to be telling us something. Later, during audio review, I found an EVP telling us, *"Amber...died."*

RECORDING

Track 14
[2 Amber Died]

After some time in Room 17, another audio clip tells of the strong Portuguese influence that the fishing industry had on Salem's history. It actually took me a little while to figure out that I was hearing Portuguese. This is a language fluently spoken in New Bedford, my hometown, which also has a strong Portuguese influence related to the fishing trade. When I finally figured it out, it made sense to me; but, at first, I was perplexed by this audio clip. I knew it was the voice of a ghost, for it was none of us, but I was listening for English words. Her inflections of the words reminded me of an older Portuguese woman asking, "How are you?" in her native tongue, *"Como estar?"*

RECORDING

Track 15
[2 Como Estar]

When I finally understood her, I wondered if she could speak or understand English. Some believe that all things are understood on the other side, but I'm not sure I can believe that myself. Many of the spirits that I've come into contact with seem to be wrapped in their own turmoil, and it begs the question whether some are capable of understanding all that much. Especially the fact that they are dead. So, I don't know if our Portuguese lady ghost could understand us or not, but it would be interesting to find out. I'd like to have a Portuguese-speaking person with us to communicate in the language this ghost probably knows best. I think it would be intriguing to see

Hoping for more physical interaction, I asked if the spirits can touch my hand. *Courtesy Crystal Washington, WCG*

what she has to say if encouraged. She seems to be friendly enough...asking how we are, after all.

Stretching out comfortably on the bed, Crystal, Gabby, and I began speculating about what spirits could be in the building. With a building as old as the Salem Inn, many things can happen. With so much history, many ghosts can get left behind.

As we used our speculations to form EVP questions, a male voice states, *"She was caught."*

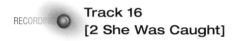

RECORDING **Track 16**
[2 She Was Caught]

I am not sure what was meant by this. I considered that it might have something to do with "Amber" from an earlier EVP clip. Wondering out loud about the woman my son had seen, I imagined her as someone who worked there, maybe as a servant to the owners of the home. Now that I've heard the Portuguese words we recorded in that room, I puzzled whether it might be the poor hunched woman—the one who walked like an elderly person instead of someone who looked much younger. Without more investigation into the matter, we won't know. (But I sure wouldn't mind getting back to the Salem Inn again; there's a jacuzzi with my name on it.)

It was getting late, and Robb and the guys were ready to call it a night. The girls and I started to wrap up the equipment we'd had running in Room 17. We were making small talk as we set about our tasks and were not actually trying to record EVP when the next audio clip came up. *"Luann,"* said by a male voice. This EVP saying my name came at almost the end of the recording for that night.

RECORDING **Track 17**
[2 Luann]

Were they sad to see us leave?

With more engagements in the enchanted city of Salem, we didn't get to investigate the Salem Inn again until two days later. It was a bit more active on that night—more about that will come later, after the telling of some exciting events in the Daniel Low building, the present-day home of Rockafellas Restaurant.

ROCKAFELLAS RESTAURANT
OFFICIAL INVESTIGATION

Our next day started early. After enjoying a delicious complimentary breakfast and lots of coffee in the Salem Inn's basement, where a delightful breakfast nook is located, we headed out to explore. We found that the trolley tour takes you around the most scenic and beautiful areas of Salem. Our driver was entertaining and funny, but, at the same time, educated us on the rich history of Salem as he pointed out landmarks to us. Even as you explore this city and hear the heartbeat of the present day all around, you can not help but hear the echoes of the past!

We headed over to Rockafellas, for we'd been invited to visit and investigate the "secret tunnels" that wind their way beneath the restaurant. On arrival, we were offered a sample of pumpkin beer to try, and were told about some of the activity surrounding the Lady in Blue.

Kevin Williams, one of the owners, explained a rumor about the Lady in Blue ghost making employees and clientele alike feel uncomfortable at times in the building. He told us that there was a rumor about a young lady who died in the building while she was working. Since the building has such a long and varied history, it is unclear as to which business she worked for at the time of her death. As I listened, my eyes could not help but look over to the portrayal of her that was painted on the wall of the dining room. The full wall mural depicts a bombshell red head in a form-fitting and sexy blue dress, backed up by a jazzy-looking band. I couldn't help but ponder whether that was her true story.

A mural adorns the wall of Rockafellas Restaurant depicting "The Lady in Blue."

Kevin explained that the Lady in Blue didn't seem to like women all that much. He told us of a female employee who the Lady in Blue would torment. This employee had complained of a force trying to push her down the stairs to the basement on several occasions. The next thing he showed us blew me away, for I had never heard of anything like it in all my years of researching the paranormal.

He took a framed photograph off the front wall of the restaurant. Looking closely at the picture, you can see a smudge of blue that seems to suggest the ghostly impression of a womanly shape. At first glance, you guess that someone took a photograph of the building outside and captured this anomaly. It is correct that someone took a picture from the outside of the building—it was taken by one of the owners. The rest is much more strange. The owner uploaded it to his work computer, and put it up as the wallpaper on his computer screen. For reasons unknown to Kevin, the owner's computer began to have problems, and it seemed as if it might crash. During the time they tried to repair the computer to get it running normally again, a strange blue dot appeared in the wallpaper picture. As the days went by, and the computer started acting more and more screwy, the blue dot on the computer wallpaper began to manifest into a human-like shape. A day or two before the computer actually did die, Kevin decided to print a picture of the wallpaper as it appeared on the computer screen. The picture you see is just as it was that day when he printed it. It can now be viewed in Rockafellas Restaurant toward the front of the building where the bar is. I find it quite amazing myself, and can't give you an explanation as to how this could have happened. Though I did ask the Lady in Blue, I never got an answer from her. But I did end up with reason to believe that the Lady in Blue doesn't really care for other women much!

Entering the subterranean tunnels beneath Rockafellas was like stepping back in time, but we also noted how conditions would make paranormal investigating a bit tricky, to say the least. Overhead, multiple electrical wires ran helter-skelter to supply the electrical needs of the kitchen and dining room.

Looking up, Robb immediately spoke up, "Fear cage," he said.

I couldn't do anything but agree, "Yeah, wicked," I told him.

In many cases, uninsulated wiring can cause a large electromagnetic field, which, in some cases, can affect the living. Extremely high EMF can cause some people to have very intense symptoms, such as paranoia, to physical symptoms, such as dizziness and vomiting. There was also a hum and lots of noise due to the restaurant's activities. We found a quieter tunnel that led to the back of the building. It was not used by any of the kitchen employees and lacked the amount of wiring that was in the main corridor. We decided this was the area where we would settle down to investigate. The conditions weren't perfect, but they were better than in the other areas of the basement. It ended up being the perfect spot to find paranormal activity in Rockafellas.

Robb and John had gone over to Kevin's office to hear more accounts of activity in the restaurant, but I felt pulled to stay in the tunnel. Greg remained behind to wander in the tunnel with me. Unfortunately, when I stood facing a ghost, with a camera that would not go off, Greg and his camera were too far away to help me document what I could *see*, but *not* take a picture of. Intrigued by this female spirit who lingered there, disliking women and feeling territorial, I kept my line of questioning in a direction that I hoped would encourage her to communicate with me.

Coming to the end of the tunnel, I found a set of stairs, going up to an exit door. I stood for a moment, and took a look through the viewfinder of Robb's camera. When I did, I saw a human-shaped shadow at the top of the stairs. I depressed the shutter button on the camera, but nothing happened. Perplexed, I looked up with my naked eyes, and saw absolutely nothing. When my eyes returned to the viewfinder, a shadowy person stood there still. Again and again, I tried to get Robb's camera to take a shot, and it refused. Just as suddenly as it appeared, the apparition seen through the viewfinder was gone. When Greg returned with the video camera, it was long gone, but we remained behind to do an EVP session. Greg taped the whole session, but the shadowy figure I saw was not spotted again. The EVP evidence, on the other hand, had some positive results—results that I have to admit, I was a little surprised about!

The EVP session lasted about half an hour, and, during that time, I do think we stirred the spirits up to respond to us. The next EVP was unexpected, for I had been anticipating the Lady in Blue to make herself known, and she did, later; but first, a male made his presence known. In this EVP clip, you can hear my voice, clearly saying, "uncomplicated," referring to Robb's camera and that it wasn't difficult to use.

Directly after that, you hear a male voice whisper, "*I'm a pipper.*"

RECORDING **Track 18**
[2 Ima Pipper]

Robb and John had rejoined Greg and me in the tunnel. I told Robb about what had happened with the shadowy apparition and he helped me continue the EVP session I had started.

While I tried to sympathize with the Lady in Blue, hoping my being female might help her to form a bond with me, Robb went in a totally different direction and tried to bring up the building's more religious side. The next EVP seems to suggest that I did get a response from the Lady in Blue, but it wasn't the response I had been hoping for (one of trust and commiseration on being female in a man's world).

Instead, she told me point-blank, amidst a strange sound that filtered in and seemed to almost sound like music: "*Now you GET!*"

RECORDING **Track 19**
[2 Now You Get]

I can not explain the strange music that seemed to filter into the recordings at times, but I *can* say it is possible it was just noise from the restaurant filtering down to us; then again, it was daytime and they weren't playing music in the bar.

Unbeknownst to us, Robb was securing a response from the spirits of male persuasion. The next EVP seems to have a bit of a religious intonation to it and could be a remnant from the days that the building housed a church.

"*Where blood is my faith*," came filtering through as Robb asked about the jewelry shop and the church.

RECORDING **Track 20**
[2 Where Blood is my Faith]

Not long after this EVP had been recorded, I sat down on the stairs to give my legs a rest. A few moments after I was seated, a steady pressure could be felt upon my right shoulder. I asked Robb to grab the thermometer and EMF detector to take readings around my body. Though the EMF did register a small reading for short bursts a few times, I can not say it was paranormal due to the amount of wiring and EMF that we had found in the basement. This makes it inconclusive, though I can say for sure that I felt a hand rest itself upon my shoulder in a friendly gesture, or so it seemed to me at the time. I think the EVP that occurred made it seem a bit more friendly, too. When the feeling had passed, I immediately set upon trying to gain some EVP evidence to go along with my personal experience. I asked who had touched me, and, after a pause, I asked if the spirit would like to touch me again. I got more replies than I expected when I reviewed the evidence. The next EVP, I have broken into pieces to bring out each piece of it more clearly.

In the original clip, you will hear me ask, "Can you touch me again?" Immediately after, a male voice answers, "*Yeah, I would!*"

RECORDING **Track 21**
[2 Yeah I Would]

With a small pause, a female voice says, "*I'm not a failure.*"

RECORDING **Track 22**
[2 I'm Not a Failure]

I felt a strong chill suddenly and asked, "Is that you making me cold?" I got a response that sounds female to me, "Who do ya think?" (Not included.) At the end of all this, a male voice asks where my son, Tyler is: "*Where's Tyler*?"

Track 23
[2 Where's Tyler]

I have no explanation as to why this spirit was asking for my son. My best guess is that we were followed by this spirit from the Salem Inn over to Rockafellas. Maybe this spirit saw me with my son at some point in our travels throughout the city. I don't think spirits are chained to the locations they haunt, so anything is possible. One thing I do know is that the spirit seemed to be interested in my son for some reason. But then again, my son is a chip off the old block.

As I kept trying to make contact with the Lady in Blue, Robb continued his line of questioning that focussed on the history that we knew of the building. He was trying to get the past owners and workers of the building, both jewelers and churchgoers alike, to respond. Equipped with a Sony Handy Cam, I moved back and forth through the tunnel, hoping that whatever apparition had appeared to me on the stairs would show itself again—and that I would be able to catch it on video.

As I moved about, Robb asked the spirit if he was a priest. There is a short pause and then a male voice answers, "*No.*"

Track 24
[2 Priest No]

I would say this is probably a correct answer. The church that was housed in the Daniel Low Building was not a Catholic church, and, as far as I know, Catholics are the only religion who employ priests as their church leaders. My guess is that whoever this spirit was must have been a reverend or a minister. From what I can gather from the history, the First Church was originally built by Puritan settlers, but, in later years, became a Unitarian church. Though the church is no longer housed in the Daniel Low Building, it seems there are remnants from the time it was located there. I can't help but wonder if this spirit knows that the church is long gone. And if he does know, why does he still linger there?

The last EVP of the day left me just as perplexed as the one asking for my son. I did ask the wonderful and helpful employees of the Salem Library to assist me with some of the research on the locations we'd investigated. They could not find a reference to the name mentioned in the following EVP, and it leaves me wondering:

Who were some of these ghosts making contact with us? We may never know, and at times, that is the nature of paranormal investigation. One sad, but true, fact is that older history was not documented as well as it is today, and many times, souls get lost along the way.

As we were leaving Rockafellas, after exploring the secret tunnels, we stopped to say goodbye to all of the staff that we had met that day. In the next EVP, you can hear a female staff member, whose voice is a bit unclear, say, "Oh, we'll keep going."

A male whisper pipes in, "*I'm Kramer.*"

RECORDING ● **Track 25**
[2 I'm Kramer]

Because of the acoustics in the building, the human voices seem a bit distorted in the recording, yet the EVP itself seems clear as a bell. Though I could not find Kramer in any documentation, I couldn't help but speculate whether he and the Lady in Blue were aware of each other in death, or if they had known each other in life. Or maybe this Kramer is our "pipper?" I hope to someday revisit Salem, and, if the conditions are right, maybe I can talk more to Kramer and the Lady in Blue to find out what their stories really are.

After lunch, we had some time to wander the shops that line the streets downtown. We found a lovely little store called The Hex Shop, and spoke to the people who worked there. As we chatted with them, we found out an interesting fact. Their medium at the shop had done a reading on the Salem Inn. I decided it would be a great chance to compare notes.

I approached the medium, LeeAnn, and asked her if she could describe any female spirits from the Inn. She was happy to and began talking about a young woman who had some type of disability in her back. She said this spirit had dark hair and shuffled when she walked. LeeAnn told me this spirit was very shy and she wasn't sure if she had been a servant in the older days of the building. I explained to LeeAnn what had happened with my son's sighting. She wasn't surprised that someone else had seen her, and I began to believe that my son had really seen something the day before. I also was hoping that I could make contact with this poor, little spirit when we returned to the Salem Inn to investigate again that night.

Acting like good tourists, we visited many of the attractions and shops that Salem boasted. We found ourselves being educated along with having one heck of a good time. We visited so many shops and museums that it was hard to keep track of them all in my head. I have to say, visit the Witch Museum and the Wax Museum. I found them not only educational, telling the story of the Witch Trials and executions, but also encouraging our next generations to be more tolerant of others who are different. I think the past tragedies that occurred in Salem have made the residents appreciate the value of hope just a bit more than those frequenting most cities, and it shines through in everything that exists today as a part of Salem. Wandering the shops and attractions like the troopers we are, we found that the whole day had passed us by. We enjoyed every minute of it and I can only say I regret that it went by so fast!

SALEM INN OFFICIAL INVESTIGATION
NIGHT TWO

Freshening up before our long night, I left my son, Tyler, in our room, and joined Robb, Greg, and John to begin setting up the equipment for the night. We decided that Room 17 was the most active. We set up infrared cameras, ran an EMF sweep, got our recorders running, checked our cameras, and settled down to investigate.

Robb discussed trying a different approach to see if we could stir up some activity. He hoped that if I couldn't get a response by being nice to the spirit, he would try a little provoking and teasing, to see if that gained a reaction. I agreed, and hoped that I could coax the little female spirit out without provocation. She just sounded delicate to me, and I wasn't sure if she would respond to teasing, or if it would scare her away. I was curious to see how any other spirits would react to Robb's approach.

Beginning the EVP session on a positive and gentle note, I tried to communicate with the female spirit that my son had seen. I asked what her name was, and if she had worked there. I would pause and ask more questions: What year was it, and had she had an accident? I spoke in a gentle voice, and told her about my son, and asked if she had ever had any children. I asked if there were other spirits with us in the room and if they could tell us their names, or make some type of sign or touch us to let us know they were there.

After a time, Robb took over the questioning and I remember laughing when he made a remark to the female spirit asking her why she

Gabby looks on as I adjust a video camera in The Salem Inn. *Courtesy Crystal Washington, WCG*

wandered around the hotel, "all old and crotchety-looking." There still seemed to be no response to either of our lines of questioning. I started checking around the room to make sure all the equipment was functioning and the recorders were still recording.

Settling back down on the bed, I noticed something in the bathroom. I wasn't sure, for I wasn't looking directly into the room, but I thought I'd seen movement. I moved around to see if it had been my own shadow, or maybe a reflection in the mirror. I didn't see anything during this experiment, so I decided that since I had to use the bathroom anyway, I'd take a closer look. When using the sink to wash my hands, I felt an intensely cold mass at my back. I dried my hands and, as I left the room, I let Robb and the crew know that there was something very cold at my back. The

Gabby trying to capture paranormal activity with her handheld video camera in Room 17 of The Salem Inn. *Courtesy Crystal Washington, WCG*

cold mass followed me into the bedroom. Robb immediately came with his EMF meter and thermometer. Though the EMF meter only went off once during the time of the cold spot, the temperature difference was quite significant. The room temperature was 74 degrees Fahrenheit, while behind me, it was 60 degrees. The temperature went down as far as 57 before it dissipated. Greg came over and could physically feel the temperature difference as he compared the air in front of me to the air behind me. The video camera did record the entire event; unfortunately, nothing was visible on the video.

After the cold spot had dissipated, I decided to try a little more EVP work. Thinking carefully about what I knew of the history, I kept forming questions. Pausing in between, I gave spirits a chance to interact with me.

When I asked if there were any spirits that wanted to communicate, I got a strange response from one male spirit. "*I can't make it,*" was his reply.

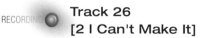

RECORDING **Track 26**
[2 I Can't Make It]

The next EVP came as a surprise to me, for when in Salem, you tend to think more of the Witch Trial events, but that's not the only bit of history that Salem can claim.

In this next clip, you hear Gabby ask if Robb would like her to check the levels, meaning EMF and temperature readings, and before Robb answers, a voice responds, *"To battle!"*

RECORDING **Track 27**
[2 To Battle]

Since I don't have more information on this spirit, I can only think that he might have meant the Revolutionary War. Most of the cities and towns, at the time, were involved with the war in one way or another, so it is safe to say that this may be what the spirit was referring to, though it's hard to be sure. The date of the Civil War is more appropriate to the age of the Salem Inn. But at times, the building itself has nothing to do with the ghosts that are present; many times, the *land* can be haunted.

The last EVP of the night, I found a bit strange and consider whether he was referring to one of the women of Whaling City Ghosts, or was he calling out for a long-lost relative.

Isolated, and not as an answer to a question, you hear, *"Mother!"* in a strong whisper.

RECORDING **Track 28**
[2 Mother]

I've reflected on who he was calling out to, and if the lady spirit my son had seen could possibly be the person he was asking for. This was clearly a Class A EVP and the intensity of the word spoken surprised me. Whatever else I hope for the spirits of Salem—peace, hope, happiness—one thing remains in my heart; and that is for this poor spirit to eventually find the mother he is looking for. I hope that they can be reunited on the other side.

As we toured the city, I couldn't help but feel the ages just beneath our feet. My heart also couldn't help but absorb the lesson that Salem teaches us. It is a simple lesson. A place can have a dark past, wrongs can be done, but we can rise above them and bring ourselves back into the light. For that is what Salem has done. They bring the rich history of a flourishing sea town to the forefront, but at the same time, they never forget the bravery of the people who would not admit they were witches, even if it meant that saying so, would have saved their lives.

In Salem, you can never forget the witch trials, but you also find so much more. I think by holding onto and learning from their past, Salem has brought so much

Gabby video taping my EVP session in Room 17. *Courtesy Crystal Washington, WCG*

light into their city that anyone visiting can not help but feel awe for everything this city represents. Being a native to this area, I've seen many seaside cities in my time, and I have to say, Salem is definitely one of my favorites!

All in all, Salem is a beautiful, well kept city with many attractions to keep a tourist busy. For a paranormal enthusiast, there are more than enough haunts to investigate. Many of the older buildings have been well kept and are accessible to the public. To leave with parting words, I give you a quote from Robb Kaczor of Other Side Paranormal Investigations:

"This city does not disappoint!"

Maybe we'll see you there some day, in the wonderful historic Witch City!

VISITOR INFORMATION

ROCKAFELLAS
231 Essex Street
Salem, MA 01970
(978) 745-2411
www.rockafellasofsalem.com

THE SALEM INN
7 Summer Street
Salem, MA 01970
(978) 741-0680
www.saleminnma.com

CHAPTER THREE

PROFILE ROCK

FREETOWN-FALL RIVER STATE FOREST AND THE CULT MURDERS

"The Sentinel." *Courtesy Crystal Washington, WCG*

OFFICIAL INVESTIGATION
JUNE 2010

Every year, our local haunted radio show, *Spooky Southcoast* does a "Bridgewater Triangle Special Edition Show" and Whaling City Ghosts is invited to investigate each year. Our first year investigating for them, we were sent to various places in the triangle, chased after the red-headed hitchhiker and visited Anawan Rock. Because of some remarkable EVP we captured at Anawan Rock, it has been a tradition to send us to visit the Wampanoag spirits at Anawan Rock. In 2010, *Spooky* decided to change things up and sent us to Profile Rock instead.

Profile Rock was once a place where King Philip, or Metacomet, went to meditate. Metacomet was the young sachem, or chief, who was left in charge of the tribe after the death of his father, and then the suspicious death of his elder brother Alexander (Wamsutta). They say the profile on the rock looks very much like his father, Massasoit, the famous chief who helped the Pilgrims to survive their first year here in America. *Spooky* sent us here because they felt that we have a special connection with the Wampanoag spirits, and they hoped that maybe we would get lucky on this night. However, Whaling City Ghosts did not meet up with the Wampanoag spirits that night. We met up with something much darker.

Profile Rock is considered part of the Freetown-Fall River State Forest in Massachusetts and is located close to the entrance of the state forest on the Slab Bridge Road side. There are miles of walking trails within

The "profile" is said to greatly resemble "Massasoit" the "Great Chief" of the Wampanoag, who helped the Pilgrims learn to live in the harsh New World and saved them from starvation. *Courtesy René Carr* the forest and many come each year to enjoy the beauty of nature. On the Profile Rock site, a trail leads to the famous rock. Other trails lead around the base, and if you are brave enough to climb to the top, the view from the rock is magnificent. Miles of forest unfold below all the way to Fall River, Massachusetts. Picturesque church steeples poke out of the tops of trees and make the view not only beautiful, but it seems to almost walk you back in time to a different, less complicated, era. Looking down from the top of Profile Rock, you'd never guess that the forest had such a dark past.

Several trails of varying difficulty lead to the spectacular view atop Profile Rock. *Courtesy René Carr*

Unfortunately, when there is such a vast amount of forest between two small cities and it is an hour away from major cities, the potential for mischief is extraordinarily high. Over the years, the area has been used as a dumping ground for evidence to crimes many, many times. It is said that dead bodies and stolen cars line the bottom of "the ledge," a deep body of water that was formed by a rock quarry that used to operate on the site. It is so deep that any evidence remains unrecoverable. But not all the bodies were dumped in the ledge; some of them were recovered, giving this beautiful place of nature a dark reputation.

Many legends and stories are told about the Freetown-Fall River State Forest. Some of them have no basis, such as the alleged native woman who has been reported as the phantom shape of a woman that throws herself over the edge, to disappear. Is it possible that she is someone else, and not a Native American woman? The quarry that operated there did not exist during the days that the Wampanoag roamed these lands.

There have been reports and a strange video taken by Christopher Balzano, author of many books (including *Dark Woods: Cults, Crime, and the Paranormal in the Freetown State Forest*) on the haunts of south eastern Massachusetts, and of the attack of a "Puckwudgie." A puckwudgie is a Native American spirit that can either be benign, or very malign, if you do not pay them proper respect. Too, there are reports of phantom campfires that recede in the distance as you try to get closer to find the source. I remember times when I was younger, riding alone on a horse through the forest, when I'd hear the whispers of the cult activity that went on there at another time and would find myself strangely nervous—suddenly feeling as if I was being watched. I never knew if the uncomfortable feeling that would make me race off at a gallop was just my imagination, or if there really was something else that lurked in the forest. Back then, I didn't know all the details of the area. It wasn't until my team came to meet some of the spirits that dwell in this deep, dark, haunted forest that I learned the macabre details of the Cult Murders.

In 1978, the body of a 15-year-old cheerleader, Mary Lou Arruda, was found tied to a tree. The body of a transient drifter was found during 1987. Two men were found shot to death in the forest on Bell Rock Road in 2001. But the most infamous murders related to the Freetown-Fall River State Forest were the Cult Murders. Brutally murdered in ritualistic fashion, three women disappeared from this realm of existence. To this day, one body has never been found, only fragments of her skull.

I believe that on the night of June 26, 2010, Whaling City Ghosts met up with the victims of these horrible crimes. And possibly, one of the murderers.

The first victim in this round of crimes was Doreen Levesque, a teenage runaway from a foster home located in New Bedford. She had been working as a prostitute in Fall River. Her body was found in October of 1979, under the bleachers of the vocational high school in Fall River. Her hands had been bound behind her back and her skull had been crushed, presumably by rocks. Her corpse had been sexually assaulted. So began the string of three grisly murders that would soon be dubbed the "Cult Murders." Did they really kill her and offer her soul to Satan? What benefits did they reap after these murders, other than jail time?

Three months later, another body was found behind a local printing shop. The corpse, found with her hands bound behind her back and her skull caved in was later identified as Barbara Raposa, also a local prostitute. The two deaths were very similar. Both had been bound, had their skulls crushed in by rocks, and had been sexually assaulted after death. The deaths had a ritualistic undertone to them, and it was believed that a Satanic Cult had been involved in the murders. I have read an account of some undercover officers who participated in a Satanic ritual, to gain entrance into the cult. They "brought the beer" and witnessed the cult members calling out, "Hail Satan!"

The final murder was by far, the most gruesome and horrible of the three murders. Karen Marsden, also a prostitute in the area, was identified by skull fragments, her hair, and jewelry. To this day, her body has never been found, and

I wonder if it ever will be. Before she was decapitated, her hair was torn from her head, her fingernails were pulled from her fingers. Her throat was then slit, and her head torn from her body, to be kicked around by the cult members who had performed her execution. An "X" was carved into her chest and later her headless body was sexually assaulted. Charged with these crimes, Robin Murphy turned state witness, giving authorities the gruesome details of Karen's murder. These rituals were performed to give the souls of the victims to Satan, and they were meant to be servants to him. But are the victims serving Satan, or wandering through the place of their death, afraid to cross over?

Peaceful forest surrounds Profile Rock by day. *Courtesy René Carr*

Three of the cult members were convicted for these crimes. Andre Maltais, the boyfriend of Barbara Raposa, who had also reported her missing three months before her body was found, was convicted of her murder. Carl Drew, a pimp, was charged in all three murders, and Robin Murphy, a prostitute/pimp was also charged. Robin Murphy turned state witness and was given a lesser sentence in exchange for testimony which helped to convict Carl Drew as the ringleader of the cult. Maltais died in prison, Carl Drew is still serving time, and, recently, Robin Murphy was released on parole. But deep in the forest, the souls of the victims of these murders still wander, prisoners of the horrendous deaths they suffered.

Whaling City Ghosts had heard of the Cult Murders, just as anyone growing up in this area had, but as we prepared for our night of investigation, they were not at the forefront of our minds. We had been assigned by *Spooky Southcoast* to go to Profile Rock to attempt to make contact with the Wampanoag spirits that may still linger—forever paying homage to the image of the great chief, Massasoit, whose likeness can be seen in the naturally formed "profile" that resides on the north face of the rock itself. We had brought some props to help us. Tobacco was to be used as an offering to the Wampanoag. René had even brought a drum to beat out a call of welcome to the spirits that we hoped we would meet that night. I was looking forward to using the Wampanoag words I had learned in hopes that hearing their native language would encourage them to come closer and possibly to communicate with us.

On an earlier date at Anawan Rock, I strongly believed that I met with Anawan, King Philip's War General. I was hoping that I would be honored by attracting King Philip himself, if only I could reach out to him. But it became apparent almost as soon as we entered the woods surrounding the rock that something else was present with us that night.

I grew up in the woods, and have always prided myself in my ability to navigate through the forests of my area confidently. I have never known fear of the animals that are native to our region and know that most of

Freetown-Fall River State Forest boasts wide trails suitable for horseback riding, off-road vehicles, and dog sledding. *Courtesy Eric LaVoie, DART*

them are more afraid of us than we are of them. Our biggest predator in the area is the coyote, and most of them have learned to stay well away from humans. Due to human predation, they are still quite rare in this area.

It wasn't the unnatural stillness in the woods or the foggy mist that filtered through the leaves, that made me uncomfortable that night. Something else did; and I couldn't, at first, place it. Many times, I have walked through the paths of the State Forest and brought my sons to Profile Rock to climb to the top. For me and my boys, these woods were always a place of light and nature. Not once during our fun-filled days in this forest had we ever felt afraid. But on this night, things were much different from the sun-showered brightness that I had grown so used to. Tonight, the darkness came not from the absence of light, but from the presence of lost souls... Souls that seemed to believe that they must now serve Satan, for all eternity.

René Carr, my Lead Investigator, and I were the only team members available on this night, and we set out into the forest with hopes of meeting some of our favorite ghosts, the Wampanoag spirits. We began our night as usual, by taking temperature and EMF readings. The full moon could not be seen because of the cloud cover and the woods were dark and still. René set up her video camera for infrared taping as I began to set up my audio recorders and check the settings on my camera. Soon after I had started my recorders, I saw a misty, human-shaped figure flit behind some trees a few yards to my right. I lost sight of it, and asked René if she could see anything in that area from her angle. She confirmed that there was nothing visible that she could report. I wondered if I had seen an apparition, or if it had been a fast-moving bank of fog. It sure had looked human shaped, so I thought it would be a good idea to watch out for more of this kind of phenomena.

As the night progressed, we both found we had the same feelings. Neither one of us believed anymore that we would be able to speak with the Wampanoag. Ever since our first contact with the Wampanoag, we had felt honored, blessed even, by their presence with us. Whatever was with us that night felt very different from what we had ever experienced when in contact with the Wampanoag, and our questioning began to change. Trying to remember as many facts as we could about the Cult Murders, we started to bring our line of questioning toward those crimes, and the victims who had been brought there to the forest to be ritualistically killed. We began to ask about the convicted murderers, and probing our memories, came up with the names of two of the victims. Without knowledge of what we were recording, we were getting responses we never dreamed of. Later, when I reviewed our audio recordings, it became apparent we had at least one of the victims present, and maybe even a murderer.

Settling myself as comfortably as I could upon the rocks that were strewn around the main base of the rock, I continued recording. René ventured out to grab a few pictures before she got down to EVP work. As the night progressed, we tried to draw up details of the Cult Murders in our minds. Framing our questions around the girls who had been killed, we slowly remembered their names. René recalled Karen

Marsden, and the fact that she knew her in younger days. A few days before Karen disappeared, René had seen her walking and she'd asked Karen if she needed a ride. Karen had declined, and later disappeared. I couldn't help but question if Karen had accepted the ride, would the outcome of her life been different? René told Karen's spirit about her little brother, as I listened close by, fascinated that René had actually known one of the victims in life. Little did we know, we'd already picked up some audio, and they didn't seem happy to see us.

As a matter of fact, a female was telling us to "*Get out.*"

RECORDING **Track 29**
[3 Get Out]

At the same time, another female was asking us to "Please come back." (Not included.) I had put the headphones on to listen to our "Hack Shack" as it continuously scanned all the frequencies without stopping on any one channel so that the spirits could use the device to "borrow" words to communicate with me (the living). As mentioned earlier, at times, it's hard to catch what is being said on the Hack Shack. The words go very fast, but I swore that I kept hearing the word "whore" as the channels sped by. I saw René was speaking and pulled the headphones off for a moment to talk with her. Shortly after that, I picked up an EVP that still sends chills down my spine. We continued our line of questioning, focused on the cult murders and the victims.

A female voice pipes in, with a sing-song tone to it and tells us, "*You will serve Satan.*"

RECORDING **Track 30**
[3 You Will Serve Satan]

I can't tell you which victim it was that made this statement, in a sweet almost childlike voice. But I can say it was a bit disturbing to think that these poor girls, murdered in such horrifying circumstances, probably believe that they must serve Satan in the afterlife. I have begun to think that this may even be why they still dwell in the forest. I know that if I thought I was to be Satan's handmaiden, I would think twice about crossing over.

René had been moving about, exploring, taking pictures, and thinking of more questions that had to do with the murders. She turned, and in the same area that I had first seen the misty figure, she saw a cloud-like, human-shaped mass move behind a tree. She called out to me and hurried over to the area where she had seen the anomaly—but to no avail. Whatever it was had disappeared. We both moved about the area, searching, but we didn't see it again. René is a great investigator; when she sees or hears something, she will search for a cause. She wandered around the trees hoping to catch a glimpse of whatever could have caused a human-shaped figure to appear to us. This time, her search was fruitless and we were left considering if it had been a bank of fog, or something else.

René and I took turns whenever we could think of more information about the Cult Murders, we framed our questions around the information we could remember. Another EVP has a male voice speaking up saying, "Some sh-- around here." (Not included.) I puzzled over exactly how many spirits were wandering the forest that night. To this day, strange things still go on in the forest that involve animal sacrifice and nighttime rituals. Through the grapevine, I have heard that the police still find these types of things are happening. Trekking in the woods, you might stumble upon altars, signs of animal sacrifice, and other evidence of Satanism.

Hiking through Freetown-Fall River State Forest, you never know what you'll find. Beautiful stonework adorns this stand-alone chimney in the middle of nowhere. *Courtesy Eric LaVoie, DART*

Not long after this contribution to the conversation from the other side, René asks, "Who is Carl Drew?" The answer is simple and states, "*Carl Drew*."

 RECORDING

Track 31
[3 Carl Drew]

In a way, I guess it makes sense, for could Carl Drew, the convicted ringleader of the cult involved in these murders, be anyone other than himself?

We continued our line of questioning, aimed at the victims of the Cult Murders. René asked if Doreen Levesque or Karen Marsden were present with us. The answer still has me confused.

The answer, "*Pregnant*," was recorded by both of our recorders, with Renés recording being a tad louder than mine.

RECORDING

Track 32
[3 Pregnant]

Could one of the girls have been pregnant at their time of death? Knowing that forensic science was not as advanced back then as it is now, we considered it possible. I reflected if it could possibly be Karen Marsden who had been with child. Her body had never been recovered, so I considered it a possibility.

Recently, I found a contact on the *Spooky Southcoast* forum who claimed to know Carl Drew. This person said that they visit him regularly in jail. They also told me that if I had any questions for Carl, that they would be happy to ask him for me. I immediately asked to relay the question of one of the girls being pregnant. When the message came back to me, Carl had stated that Barbara Raposa had been pregnant at her time of death. I have no way to confirm this, I can only take the word of a convicted murderer. One who claims innocence, and reports that he was just as much a victim of this cult as the victims of murder were. I can only hope that if he is truly innocent that justice is served in the end.

René got up to take some pictures; as she walked away I heard a noise. It sounded like something bouncing off of something else. A small thud followed by another as something hit the ground. René exclaimed that a stick had just hit her on the back of her leg. I came immediately to look around and did find a stick on the ground. We both experimented with it, turning it this way and that and stomping on it to see if we could recreate what we'd heard/felt. Neither one of us was successful at making the stick move very much.

Just then, the phone rang; *Spooky Southcoast* was calling in to check on how we were doing out in the woods, all alone. As I chatted with them and tried to make the show enjoyable with our stories of dark woods and misty figures, René reminded me to tell the radio show that something had thrown a stick at her. In between this and my laughter, and accusing the *Spooky Crew* of trying to get us killed by asking if we'd climbed Profile Rock in the pitch darkness, a female sounding voice chimes in saying, "I did!" (Not included.) I can't help but appreciate an honest ghost, but it didn't give us much information as to which spirit had actually thrown the stick at René. Or why. Did the spirit want René's attention? For us to know that she was there? Or did she want us to leave? I'm hoping that the spirits there simply wanted our attention, and that maybe on further investigations in the Freetown-Fall River State Forest/Profile Rock will lead us to more answers on this especially brutal case.

The last EVP of the night gave us more evidence that we may be dealing with the Cult Murder case.

As mentioned, René knew Karen in life, and to this day, knows a member of her family. She spoke to Karen about this relative and brought her up to date on present days. She also asked victim Doreen (Levesque) many questions. Alone in the darkness of the forest, surrounded by mist and trees, and not a single living thing, the murders seem so much closer, so much more frightening.

So to hear one of the victim's names called out makes it that much more real. The last EVP for this location was the name, "*Doreen*," and I do believe that it was referring to Doreen Levesque. I'm not sure if it says "who" or "ooo" just before the name, but I am sure that the EVP says the name Doreen.

RECORDING **Track 33**
[3 Doreen]

The full moon was peeking through the clouds as we began to break down our equipment. Crickets began to sing, and I realized that this was what had been missing most of the night. Their silence made me wonder if they feared the spirits that wander the woods. On any given night in June, frogs and crickets usually serenade you with their songs. During our time at Profile Rock, the woods had been still and silent and I kept trying to identify what it was that seemed "off" to me. It wasn't until I heard them that I realized it was the usual night noises I'd been listening for. Was it our presence that stilled their calls, or was it the presence of something else that quieted them? I can't say, but I do know that, as the moon stared down at us, the woods suddenly came alive with the sounds of life. Were crickets and frogs able to see things that our human eyes could not? Did they fear ghosts? Still I can't answer, but as their songs followed us out of the woods, I have to say they didn't show much fear for the living.

René and I were so affected by the audio we recorded that night, we have promised ourselves we would return to learn as much as we could about this case. We have also decided that if something can be done to help these lost, tortured souls, that we will try.

I expect that, with the permission of the Town of Freetown, we will be returning often. There seems to be something dark lurking in the Freetown State Forest/Profile Rock area. During the day, it is a beautiful example of New England forest land, with miles of trails and the monument of Profile Rock that tells of the Wampanoag influence over this area. But, by night, it is the home of lost souls. Souls that I can't help think they may know that they still have a choice, but are too afraid to make it. Are they afraid Satan is waiting just beyond the edge of the other side?

A "Pet Sematary" hidden amongst the trees is a strange and creepy place to stumble upon.
Courtesy Eric LaVoie, DART

Every single day on this planet, crimes are committed. Some of them are even more brutal than these crimes that occurred decades ago in the Freetown-Fall River State Forest. Does that mean that every victim of murder is caught here, betwixt and between the worlds? Or do some of them, freed of the chains that bind them to this realm fly free to the other side? Is there a Heaven? Is there a Hell? Even if there is, shouldn't there be forgiveness for the souls of victims who never asked for the ways they met their ends? If there is forgiveness in the great scheme of things, then why don't the souls of these poor girls find it? Can your last thoughts, your last grasp at this life cause you to be trapped here forever? Can what you believed at the moment of your death carry on after you have left your living body behind?

Meeting the victims of the Cult Murders only gave me more questions. I do know one thing, these girls have touched my heart in ways I can never explain. For as a woman, I am at the mercy of this world and the people in it. My end could easily be as horrifying as these women, or so many other victims who have perished at the hands of others. If I did meet with such a horrible end, would I be trapped here, forever searching for what I lost? I can only hope not. Whatever it is that binds these spirits to this earth, I hope that my soul looks to death as a ticket to fly free! I bet there's a lot to explore on the other side!

As long as I live, I will always be haunted by that seemingly sweet voice that rang through the forest on the night of our investigation. I have often thought on the fairness of this situation. Was it fair for these girls' lives to be snuffed out before they had even begun? It seems even less fair to me that these tortured souls still wander the forest, looking for, what, I don't know. Do they truly believe that in crossing over they will be forced to serve Satan? Or do they already serve him by haunting the deep, dark woods of the Freetown-Fall River State Forest? You do know what I'm going to say, don't you? Only time, more research, and more investigations will tell!

If you'd like to visit Freetown-Fall River State Forest, I highly recommend it! If you don't come for the ghosts, come for the miles of trails and the beauty of a New England forest. Horseback riding, off road vehicles, hunting and fishing are allowed in the park. It is open year round, during the daylight hours, but nighttime passes can be obtained through the office located at the entrance to the park. If you like rock climbing, head up the road a bit and you'll find Profile Rock. If you make it to the top of the rock, I think you'll appreciate the view as much as I do.

Just remember to tell "our girls" that Whaling City Ghosts says hi!

TIP

If you decide to pursue ghost hunting as a hobby or serious endeavor, always pair up with another person. Ghost hunting alone can be dangerous. Not only do you open yourself to attack, but if you were injured, there would be no one to help you! Please stay safe!

VISITOR INFORMATION

FREETOWN-FALL RIVER STATE FOREST
Slab Bridge Road
Assonet, MA 02743
508-644-5522

CHAPTER FOUR

LIZZIE BORDEN'S
BED & BREAKFAST

"Gaited Community." *Courtesy Crystal Washington, WCG*

LIZZIE BORDEN TOOK AN AXE
AND GAVE HER MOTHER FORTY WHACKS.
WHEN SHE SAW WHAT SHE HAD DONE
SHE GAVE HER FATHER FORTY-ONE.

Lizzie Borden stares down at guests
as they visit her home. *Courtesy Crystal
Washington, WCG*

OFFICIAL INVESTIGATION
MARCH 2007

Lizzie Borden is a figure shrouded by mystery. On August 4, 1892, Andrew Borden, Lizzie's father, and Abigail Borden, Lizzie's step-mother, were found dead in their home. A week later, Lizzie was arrested for the crimes. Yet almost a year later, on June 20, 1893, she was acquitted and set free. There are many theories concerning one of the most infamous murder cases in New England history, but so far, it still remains an unsolved crime.

After meeting Lizzie and her family, I find myself siding with Lizzie. This house is a hotbed of paranormal activity and some of the activity I've witnessed still has me wondering. Having grown up knowing the twisted jump rope song which tells of eighty-one whacks with an ax, I've always felt there was something missing in this case. In all actuality, there were approximately eighteen blows to Abigail's head and eleven to Andrew's. Not to say that they weren't still fatal, no matter what count you give them. But no matter how many blows to the head, or who did it, the spirits do not rest easy at Lizzie's house.

There are probably as many theories as there are suspects in this case. Andrew Borden was a banker, he had money, and so, he had enemies. He also had family, including an alleged illegitimate son. Any number of them, or possibly a family-wide conspiracy, could have been responsible for the murders. There are even numerous rumors that Andrew fed his family rotten food to save money, as he was a penny pincher in the extreme. There are also rumors that he may have molested Lizzie. So many theories, with no proof.

But the murders and all the twists and turns to this mystery aren't what concern me. It's the complex interplay of the lingering spirits in the house that draws my attention—spirits of yesterday, lurking, playing out dramas that have long since passed.

Investigations at Lizzie's house are always pretty lively, considering the people there are dead. Whaling City Ghosts has investigated the house several times over the years and I am convinced that not only are the Bordens alive and kicking—well, sort of—they also have some house guests that never checked out. Along with the Borden family, there are reports of at least four ghostly children who frequent the house. Two of the child spirits were victims of drowning—in a well, put there by their own mother. She then entered the house next door to her own, which later became the Borden home, and slit her own throat... Or so the story goes.

Is it a strange twist of fate or a coincidence that these children and their mother were related to the Bordens? Recently, Debby White-Paiva looked into this legend and found that though the mother did drown her children in a cistern, and did indeed slice her own throat with her husband's straight razor after committing this foul deed, it all happened next door in her own home. We found that one of the children, the oldest, who was four at the time, Maria Borden, did survive. Lucky for her, she wasn't home when this incident happened. She married a Hinckley; after his death she remarried to a Chase and resided in the house next to Lizzie until a year or so before the infamous ax murders. The other children have not been identified as far as I know, but many think they come to play with the remaining children in the home. There's even been reports of a ghost cat being seen in this house, which is now a bed and breakfast/museum. The owners, managers, and workers claim that it is very haunted by the spirits of the Bordens and other, unknown spirits.

During investigations at Lizzie Borden's, Whaling City Ghosts and other teams we've worked with have recovered evidence to back the claims up. On our first investigation there, we joined Shadow Land Investigators from Michigan: Robb Kaczor, Joan St. John and Charla White. Tim Weisberg, Matt Costa (the "Silent Assassin"), and Matt Moniz (better known as the "*Spooky Crew*" from the local radio show *Spooky Southcoast)* also joined us for the night. It was great to have them with us, for if anyone knows of the paranormal activity in Lizzie's, it's the *Spooky Crew*!

Entering Lizzie Borden's Bed & Breakfast for the first time is like walking into history. The house has been decorated to match the Victorian era appointments

Andrew Borden didn't look any less stern in his younger days. *Courtesy Crystal Washington, WCG*

of Lizzie's time. Pictures of the Borden family hang on the walls. Mr. Borden looks down upon you with disdain in his gaze. Behind glass, in the dining room, are pictures of the skulls that were once held up in the courtroom, causing Lizzie to faint. Pictures of the murder scene show the violence of the crimes: Andrew Borden, splayed across the sofa he had lain upon to take a nap, Abigail Borden facedown on the floor. In Andrew's photograph, you can just make out the fact that half of his face has been bludgeoned away. Looking at these photos, you can't imagine that Lizzie did it. Could you?

For the first hour or so, we busied ourselves with setting up multiple cameras to record video. Gabby and I ran EMF and temperature sweeps of the entire house, from basement to third floor. We did note that fuse boxes in the first floor hallway, near the front stairs, and the one in the cellar were throwing quite high readings. Temperatures ran from the high sixties to low seventies throughout the house. When the equipment was set up to our liking, and our reading sweeps were finished, we got down to investigating the paranormal activity in the house.

Tim Weisberg, the host of *Spooky Southcoast,* had investigated the home before and knew all the "hot spots" of interest. He took us first to the room where Abigail Borden was found dead, known as the John Morse Room. It is where John Morse, Lizzie's and her

Lee-ann Wilber, a co-owner and manager of Lizzie Borden's Bed & Breakfast/Museum has painstakingly restored the home with period appropriate furnishings. *Courtesy Crystal Washington, WCG*

sister Emma's uncle, had been staying for a few days around the time the murders occurred. Abby must have been in the process of cleaning up the room, while Mr. Morse was out for the day, when the ax murderer crept up behind her.

Tim explained to us a strange phenomenon that occurs when one stood between the mirrored dresser and the bed. For some reason, in this spot, some force pushes a person to the point of overbalancing. He demonstrated while calling out to Mr. Borden in ways that would provoke him. Tim also explained that it seemed as if Mr. Borden had a strong dislike for him and that he usually reacted violently when Tim called him out. (I'd say Tim was probably right in that aspect. I also had reason to believe that Mr. Borden didn't like me very much either, but that comes later.) While

The area where Abby's body was found and where strange phenomena occurs. *Courtesy Crystal Washington, WCG*

watching Tim closely, we all noted that it did seem as though something was pushing him over. Matt Costa tried this, but did not get the resultant push. When Matt Moniz tried it, something seemed to push him. Gabby, of Whaling City Ghosts, tried it and was also pushed. (I did not try this until a later investigation.)

While Matt Moniz was being "pushed" by an unseen force, Tim Weisberg had asked if Abby was the one doing the pushing. In the recording, you can hear Tim asking the question, Moniz making a noise as he's being pushed, and then a female spirit answering, "*Don't*."

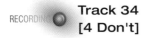

Track 34
[4 Don't]

Shortly after, we all hear a bang; Gabby asked if the noise came from the spirits. A short time after that, we move around a bit, which can be heard as a creaking, and then a female spirit says, "*That's not us*."

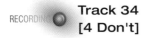

Track 35
[4 That's Not Us]

Later, as I reviewed the audio recordings, I was shocked at the apparently aware responses we'd gotten.

We had all settled down to do a bit of recording in the Abby murder room, when Tim mentioned that Abby didn't like it when anyone spoke of the murders. We began to ask questions about that day, and the murders. I later found this recording, which I found remarkable for its length, but also its content. While we sat questioning, oblivious to her voice, a female spirit made this statement, "*Oh jeesh, there's a man in the hall, watch the murderers repent*."

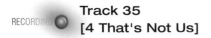

Track 36
[4 Man in the Hall Murderers Repent]

I have to admit, as I was editing this recording, and it dawned on me what it said, I was blown away. This one statement brings into account the thought of more than one person perpetrating the crimes. But who said it? Was it Abby? And is it the truth? Could she have been talking about murderers in general? The mother who drowned her children could also be called a murderer in her own right. I may never know who or what she meant.

Not long after, I was feeling a bit uncomfortable for no reason. I asked why Abby didn't want to talk about the murders. It appeared as if Tim was right that Abby didn't like to talk about that, for after I asked about them, a female voice responds, *"Go away!"*

RECORDING
Track 37
[4 Go Away]

Listen carefully to this recording; you'll hear my voice, and then the EVP itself is very quick, occurring directly after my voice. Hearing her response in my evidence justified what Tim had told us, and made me feel a little guilty for pushing it. Abby seemed willing enough to speak, as long as I didn't push her to talk of the day she was murdered with an ax. I can't say that I blame her; I'm not sure how I would feel if I was murdered in that way. Though we didn't hear Abby tell us to go away, we did just that—moving to the third floor, to the "chimney room" or the Hosea Knowlton Room.

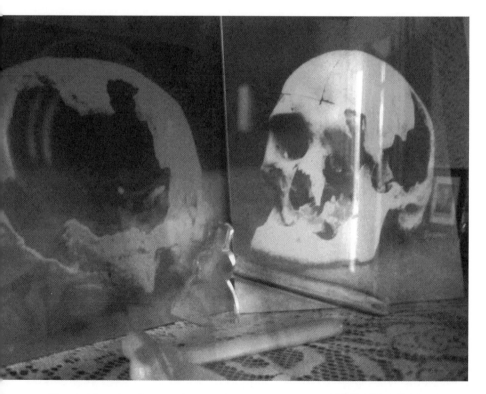

Hosea Knowlton is most famous for being the chief prosecutor in the trial of Lizzie Borden. This room, also known as the "chimney room," has a chimney running

Pictures of Andrew and Abigail's skulls show the violence of the crimes.
Courtesy Crystal Washington, WCG

through the center of the room. An antique chest sits in one corner, and the bed is covered with a patchwork quilt. It seems like such a peaceful place, who would guess that some amazing EVP comes from this room? Or that some spirit lurks under the bed, waiting to grab your legs?

After we'd settled into position, Tim Weisberg demonstrated the strange phenomenon that occurred when someone lies on the bed, with legs hanging over the side. Tim kept goading the spirit on, telling it to lift his legs, and finally it did. Something grasped his leg, then raised it as high as the side of the bed. When Gabby tried it, her legs were not lifted, but she did mention that she felt funny.

In the recording something says, *"Come on."*

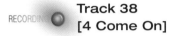

Track 38
[4 Come On]

Right after this is when Gabby stated that she felt funny.

I also tried the leg lifting out for myself. As I laid on the bed, Tim called out to the spirit and told it to lift my legs. I helped, also asking it to lift my legs. As I laid there waiting, something, like an unseen hand, clamped around my leg. My pant leg was suddenly plastered against my calf. Though it was visible to our naked eyes, it was not visible in the video, due to the infrared not being as clear as normal video. But we did all witness this, and I know I felt that unseen hand wrapped around my leg.

Shortly after this, unbeknownst to us, we recorded what sounds like a child saying the name, *"David."*

RECORDING

Track 39
[4 David]

You hear my voice as I hesitate to answer a question, "Um," followed by the EVP. Soon after, a last name follows, "Tinkham" (not included), so I believe these two clips may make a full name. After hearing this, I wondered if it could be the spirit of a child hiding under the bed and grabbing legs. It does seem a childish prank to play. After hearing recordings from our next investigation, I wasn't so sure. Then, as we switched up leg-pulling victims, an EVP recording tells us to "Give it up." (Not included.)

We decided to end the investigation, and as we were leaving the room, Tim said that he guessed we'd have to "call it a night." You can hear us all moving as a female voice calls out the word, "Heaven." (Not included.) I can only speculate if that is the place she'd like to be.

OFFICIAL INVESTIGATION
AUGUST 2007

We returned to Lizzie's on August 8, 2007, by invitation from the *Spooky Crew*, to help *SoCo Magazine* with a story they had planned for their October 2007 edition. The subject of the story involved staying in a haunted house for a night. I think the writer, Bob Ekstrom, wanted to see a paranormal investigation firsthand. We were eager to help out, and more than ready to investigate Lizzie's again. We were intrigued with the EVPs we'd recorded on our prior visit, and hoped we'd be successful in recovering more evidence of the spirits there. The ghosts of Lizzie's house did not disappoint us.

Before going on the investigation, Gabby and I had prepared to try something new. We picked out crystals that had protective qualities and put them in our pockets. We wanted to experiment with them, for we'd both read that certain crystals have certain qualities. For example, some crystals are used by healers and other crystals are supposed to help heighten psychic abilities. Still others have calming properties, and some can allegedly absorb negative energies and vibrations. We thought it would be interesting to see if these crystals lived up to their purported properties. We were very surprised at how the spirits reacted to them.

Almost as soon as we entered the house, the spirits let us know how they felt about the rocks in our pockets. In this recording, you hear Matt Moniz ask, "Gabby would you..." and Gabby stating that she has a dirty feeling. While they are talking, something else is, too. In the recording you will hear, "*She has rocks...*" a pause, then, "*...has rocks like knives.*"

RECORDING ● **Track 40**
[4 She Has Rocks Rocks Like Knives]

To me, it sounds like two separate spirits making separate, but related, comments. The phrases sound as if there is a male spirit speaking first, and then a female. Either way, I do believe the spirits were talking about the crystals we had been carrying in our pockets that night. It also gives credence to the protective properties of crystals. Gabby and I never leave home without them now.

We began the night in the Hosea Knowlton Room on the third floor. Tim demonstrated the leg lifting game, but without the usual results. His leg wasn't coming up very high this time. Tim decided to try to provoke the spirit and make it angry to see if it would lift his leg higher.

I asked Gabby a question and she replied, "I think so," yet a spirit didn't agree with her. In the recording, directly after Gabby speaks, a voice disagrees with her, "I don't think so." (Not included.) At the end, you hear Tim demanding that the spirit tell us its name. I had to wonder if this entity was being sarcastic. As we watched Tim on the bed, he asks if the spirit wants some more. It answers him and says, *"More, yeah."*

RECORDING
Track 41
[4 More Yeah]

Tonight, the spirit under the bed was not cooperating with Tim as it usually did. He kept trying different ways to provoke it into lifting his leg higher. He asked the spirit if it wanted to pick up his leg again, and the spirit, apparently provoked into anger, says, *"Why don't you go f--- yourself?"*

RECORDING
Track 42
[4 Why Don't You Go F Yourself]

Later, as I shared this evidence with *Spooky Southcoast,* it gained the title "Spookiest EVP" *Spooky Southcoast* had ever heard. As I recovered this EVP from the recording, I couldn't help but laugh. Tim had done a good job provoking the spirit's anger, whether he knew it or not.

Later, some of the EVP from this investigation was used for the TV show *My Ghost Story* and I found cause to go back to have a listen. Something made me think to turn the EVP around and play it backwards. I'd recently heard reports that Lee-ann, the owner, was being attacked in the house.

The house is beautiful, restored to its former look when a wealthy banking family had lived there in the late 1800s. At the same time, there has always seemed to be a darker side. I have to admit I wasn't all that surprised when some of the EVP from Lizzie's also clearly said something when played in reverse. "Why don't you go F yourself," became, *"We want more information,"* when played backward.

RECORDING
Track 43
[4 Why Don't You Go F Yourself Reversed]

When an EVP is played in reverse, providing understandable words, this is usually the sign of a negative entity. I have experimented with many of my EVPs over the years. The ones that I truly believe to be human spirits don't make sense when you play them in reverse, sounding like random noise. With certain more negative EVP, once reversed, they make clear sense, and, at times, can be threatening in nature.

Again, I'm left wondering about these negative entities and why so little research has been done on them. I know I've lived through a terrible negative haunt; I've seen others suffer through them. I can only hope that more study will be conducted concerning these cases and that we find answers that will help people, like myself, and so many others out there.

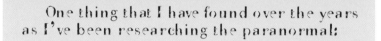

TIP

One thing that I have found over the years as I've been researching the paranormal:

If there is a large number of human spirits in a home or property, there is usually at least one negative entity among them. Do they feed off the pain and suffering of lost souls? Do they hold them here, trapped by their negative power? I have no answer for you, but I promise I will continue to look for answers!

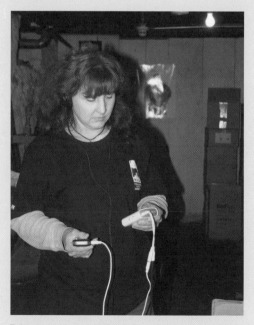

Trying out my new toy, the *Spooky Crew's* "Cellphone to the Dead" in the basement of Lizzie's house. *Courtesy Crystal Washington, WCG*

I captured a strange, moving mist in the basement using Robb Kaczor's (OSPI) camera.

A second shot of the moving mist in the basement of Lizzie's.

Third and final shot of the moving mist in Lizzie's basement. Could it have been something paranormal in this hotbed of activity?

Not long after, Gabby had turned on her camera, which has a distinctive musical sound. The spirits must have been puzzled with the noise, for one asks, "What is that?" (Not included.) As Tim was still provoking the bed spirit, we didn't even notice Gabby's camera sound.

Tim was really getting into his provocation and tells the spirit, "Pick them up you son of a b----!" The spirit must have thought this was rude for Tim to swear at it, even if it had sworn at him, for it says, *"Hey buddy!"*

RECORDING

**Track 44
[4 Hey Buddy]**

It wasn't until later, when the evidence was reviewed that I found these clips, but when I did, I was very pleased with the apparent interactive EVP that had been recorded. Shortly after, we moved down to the Abby murder room.

The John Morse Room, where Abby was murdered, looks, today, almost exactly like the photographs of the murder scene. It has been furnished with a heavy wood-framed bed and mirrored dresser that closely match the one that was there the day Abby faced her murderer(s). Since there is a wound on her face, I have to believe that, at some point, she turned, and saw who was killing her.

As I've investigated this home more than once, I have come to believe that there are more than just the Bordens here. I can only think that this house holds more spirits than meets the eye. It also makes me wonder if there is such a thing as a "vortex," or opening that spirits can travel through easily.

Many theories come into play when investigating the Borden house. South eastern New England sits on the coast of the Atlantic Ocean, so we have the conductivity of water to contend with. This area was also known for its high-quality granite, which has a high crystal quartz content. Many believe that water helps conduct needed energy for spirits to manifest. It is also believed that crystal quartz has the potential to store energy, which spirits can also use to manifest. I later came to ponder: Do the contaminants in the area help the spirits to manifest in locations that have been saturated with them? Working closely with Debby White-Paiva on this, she found that many of our most active haunts are on, or close to, super-fund sites, where clean up of contaminants are performed before houses are built.

Maybe misery just likes company, and when more than one spirit is present, others will congregate. I do not have an explanation as to why this seems to be true, but I have noted, over the years, that where more than one spirit is present, others seem to be drawn there. This is not always true, and I do have to accept the fact that maybe some of the spirits we hear at locations are in places they don't belong, or that they could be "followers." These are spirits that are attached to a living person and seem to follow them everywhere they go. Maybe one or more of the investigators have a spirit, or more, following them, and then we sometimes gain evidence of them.

I believe that in Lizzie's case, some of the spirits are Bordens, or closely related to them or the murder case. But as for the children and other spirits recorded in the house, I do not know why they are residing there with the Borden family. Only more time and research on this house will tell.

I'm left guessing about this next EVP and what this spirit means about "getting involved" but maybe you will have an idea that I haven't thought of as you listen. You'll hear the beep of our equipment and Matt Moniz murmuring in the background, then, "*Get involved*."

RECORDI ⬤ **Track 45**
[4 Get Involved]

Ever since I was a little girl and heard the jump rope song about the forty whacks, I couldn't believe that Lizzie Borden had killed her two parents in cold blood. I couldn't imagine bludgeoning someone to death in such a manner. I hadn't known much about the case—I'd only heard the song—and when I'd asked my parents about it, they told me very little. They didn't know much about it themselves, though of course, they'd heard of it. I knew someone had killed the Bordens with an ax, that Lizzie had been arrested for the crimes, but later acquitted of the charges. I felt sorry for Lizzie, and the ordeal she'd gone through, for I never believed she did it. I believed that money had to be involved, but even so, I *still* couldn't believe Lizzie had done it. I can't give you a rational answer as to why I thought this. Now as an adult, I've come to think that though Lizzie didn't pick up the ax (and I don't believe that she really did), I believe it was a conspiracy that she knew about.

There are little things that make me think it was a family-wide conspiracy. For one, John Morse, Lizzie's uncle, seems to have too good of an alibi. He could recall every single trolley he'd been on by number, and even recalled badge numbers of police officers he'd walked by on his outing. Either he had a photographic memory to the extreme, or, he purposely noted these things—for when they'd be needed later. It also seems to me as if Lizzie tried to get herself and Bridget Sullivan, the maid, out of the house that day. It is said that Lizzie tried to get the maid to go shopping for calico cloth with her, but was unsuccessful because Bridget was not feeling well that day. I think Lizzie tried to set herself up with an alibi, but was too loyal to the woman who served her family to leave her alone in the house, knowing what was to occur. It is my thought that she believed that she would never be suspected. Maybe she was even in the house that day and witnessed the murders, and so had to burn her dress, as was noted in the case. Just close enough to get a little blood on her, but never picking up an ax. Since the dress was burned by Lizzie herself, we'll never know for sure if it was blood, or paint as she claimed.

Maybe I'm wrong about Lizzie. Maybe she *was* a homicidal maniac, who picked up an ax and bashed her parents to death with it. This next piece of audio will make you think about that. It sure makes me wonder. If only we could get in a time machine and witness the events of August 4, 1892, maybe Lizzie would tell us. Or maybe she already has.

In this clip, we were still in the Abby murder room. We'd been doing an EVP session for a bit and explaining to the *SoCo* writer, Bob Ekstrom, what types of activity occurred in this room. At this point, we were silent, though you can hear my camera go off, then you hear a female voice with a Victorian era accent declare, "*I'm a good daughter!*"

RECORDING ● **Track 46**
[4 I'm a Good Daughter]

By itself, it is a startling piece of evidence, coming from where it does in the house. Coupled with the other audio clip recorded on an earlier investigation, I think it makes amazing evidence. If Abby says, "Oh jeesh, there's a man in the hall; watch the murderers repent," while Lizzie says, "I'm a good daughter," what does that say for this case? I think it proclaims that even if Lizzie was involved in a conspiracy, I don't think she ever picked up a weapon against her parents. Maybe she even felt justified in what she was doing that day. We don't know what Lizzie lived through in that house, or how harshly she was treated. Maybe Lizzie had her reasons, if she was indeed involved at all. She did stand to inherit, and, in fact, received an inheritance after she was released from jail. But was her inheritance the reason for the murders? Was it her father's abuse? I wonder if we'll ever know. I can only hope to investigate this home further and gain more evidence relative to the case. Maybe Lizzie will tell me!

For many years, I felt as if this EVP was Lizzie Borden herself, proclaiming her innocence. Now I am not so sure. Again, prompted by what I'd seen on *"My Ghost Story"* in which Tim Weisberg and Jeff Belanger borrowed some of my EVPs from previous investigations, I took this EVP and reversed it. I was shocked! I remember feeling my stomach drop out from beneath me. Everything I thought I knew about Lizzie Borden, and her innocence that I believed in, came crashing down. I could no longer believe that this was a recording of Lizzie Borden's voice. When *"I'm a good daughter"* is reversed, the EVP sounds like a woman's voice, Victorian accent and all, screaming, *"My daughter was raped."*

RECORDING ● **Track 47**
[4 I'm a Good Daughter Reversed My Daughter Was Raped]

I find it highly unlikely that the *"good daughter"* EVP is even a human spirit. Though not all of the EVP from Lizzie Borden's house can be played backward, this was enough to make me reflect upon just what was going on at the Lizzie Borden Bed & Breakfast.

Oblivious to the recordings that I'd uncovered when I reviewed the evidence, we continued our investigation in the Abby murder room. This time, I tried the push spot. I knew that something would push the person standing in between the bed and the mirrored bureau, right where they found Abby's body. I tried many stances to ensure that I was standing solidly and not letting my weight tip. I'd close my eyes, and wait, and suddenly would feel a bit like I was overbalancing. As I did, I began to ask Abby questions about the murders and telling Mr. Borden that I didn't care for him that much. Suddenly, I felt as if the right side of my face was burning. I let everyone know this, and asked Gabby to take a temperature reading of the two sides of my face. We had inadvertently left our digital thermometer upstairs, and Gabby ran for it. The sensation peaked, and it felt as if I was being branded with a hot iron; it was quite painful for a moment. Then the sensation faded. Gabby got back to the room and found that there was a five degree temperature difference between the two sides of my face. I'm sure it would have been much higher if she'd arrived earlier. My face was slightly pink on the right side where I'd felt the burning sensation, but it did fade quickly and there was no permanent mark or burn to speak of.

Shortly after this event, the audio recordings revealed a strange EVP. Tim Weisberg can be heard making note of a gum wrapper he'd just crumbled. An entity speaks just after this, saying, *"I'm Anvelo...ha..ha...ha!"*

RECORDING

Track 48
[4 I'm Anvelo]

Another spirit, apparently answering this statement, says, *"Yes, too bad for them."*

RECORDING

Track 49
[4 Yes Too Bad For Them]

I can only wonder who this "Anvelo" is and why it's too bad for us that he's there. Maybe he is the prankster who lifts legs and swore at Tim. Or could it be there is some condition that exists at this location that attracts other spirits, and this is just one of them? Was this the spirit that burned my face, while I was thinking it was Andrew? I must note here that after the episode of *"My Ghost Story,"* this recording, *"Anvelo"* is one of the EVPs that I decided to try and reverse. It sounds like either, "I'm a devil" or "I'm a bad one." (Not included.)

We went back to provoking Mr. Borden at this point. Or at least Tim did. He asked many questions about the rumors we'd all heard. He asked if Mr. Borden fed his family rotten meat...if he had molested his daughter, Lizzie...if she had been pregnant and the baby had been "taken care of."

Tim then asked if Mr. Borden had any questions for us. The answer from one spirit was, *"Not now,"* while another says, *"Yes!"*

 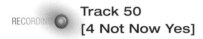 **Track 50**
[4 Not Now Yes]

Oblivious to what the spirits said, Tim goes on to provoke Mr. Borden more. He calls him Andy, then Andrew. Then he states that as much as he knows about those involved now, he doesn't have a lot of respect for them. A female spirit answers, *"We need more."*

René Carr enjoys a night with Lizzie Borden and *The Spooky Crew. Courtesy Crystal Washington, WCG*

  Track 51
[4 We Need More]

Does she mean the spirits want more living humans to visit? In this house, I think anything is possible!

Again, I was prompted by the TV show to rethink some of the EVPs that had been recorded. When reversed, *"We need more,"* becomes, *"How are you?"*

Track 52
[4 We Need More Reverse How Are You]

Strange how the female voice seemed calm and inquiring as it asked, in reverse, how we were. I've played with many recordings over the years, slowing them, reversing them; and most times, as I mentioned earlier, reversing the recording only sounds like noise. I've gone so far as to record my own voice saying a phrase and then playing it backward. The sounds my own recording makes in reverse seldom sound human, but more like plain-old *noise*. I can't explain how it's possible for these recordings to be so clear when reversed. I do feel it should be experimented with much more.

Tim Weisberg went on with his provocation of Mr. Borden and what I next witnessed still has me perplexed. Tim stood in between the bed and the wall and told Mr. Borden that he knew he didn't like him. He told Mr. Borden that the feeling was mutual. Tim went on to say that he couldn't respect a man who would feed his family rotten meat and who would molest his own daughter. The atmosphere in the room became charged. I watched as Tim shouted at Mr. Borden to, "Go ahead and hit me!" Slowly but surely, Tim was battered against the wall. First one shoulder, then the other was visibly pushed backward violently. We all took many pictures of this event, but whatever was pushing Tim against the wall didn't show up in any of them. I still have to ask the question: Was it Anvelo or Mr. Borden? Whoever was responsible, it was probably one of the strongest paranormal events I'd ever witnessed.

Later in the night, we all were taking a well-deserved break on the third floor. We were just outside the Hosea Knowlton Room talking and watching the TV monitor that was hooked up to a small infrared camera that Matt Moniz had placed on the chest that sits in the corner of the room. As we spoke, suddenly the camera turned, pointing downward to the legs of the staff of Lizzie Borden's house.

I immediately went into the room and tried to determine if one of the staff had inadvertently stepped on a wire and caused the camera to move. I found that they stood approximately three feet away from where the wires were taped down with duct tape. I then tried moving the wires with my own feet, dragging my shoes over them. I got closer and tugged on the wires with my hand. Matt Moniz asked me to step on the wires again, and I literally danced on them, but to no avail; the camera did not move. The only way I could make the camera move was by grabbing the unit itself and turning it.

With Matt guiding me in amusing, colorful terms, I adjusted the camera back to its previous position. I shut off my flashlight and found myself blinded by the light change. Just as my eyes were trying to adjust to the darkness, the camera suddenly moved on its own again, pointing right at my legs. I again went through all the motions, trying to make the camera move on its own, but could not do it. We re-adjusted the camera again and waited, but the camera remained stationary and did not move again that night.

This footage was shown on *Monster Quest* and can still be viewed online. It is called the "Ghosts" episode. To this day, I can not give an explanation as to why the camera moved by itself, unless I say it was a spirit that moved it.

LIZZIE'S SPOOKY NIGHT
APRIL 2008

By invitation of a friend, I joined the *Spooky Southcoast* Lizzie Borden's Investigator's Night. On this night, the *Spooky* Crew, Tim Weisberg, Matt Costa, and Matt Moniz had teamed up with Lizzie Borden's Bed & Breakfast to have an open night for the public to join investigators and for teams to investigate the paranormal activity that occurs in this inn/museum. For myself and Crystal Washington, a new member of my team, it was a chance to have some fun and relax from the strict discipline we normally display on investigations.

I enjoyed myself, socializing and playing with the *Spooky Crew's* new toy they had made, which they called the "Cell Phone to the Dead." It is basically a spin off of the Frank's Box which is used to scan radio frequencies, and, therefore, the theory is that spirits can use this energy to communicate with us live. Well, sort of. At one point, with the headphones still on my head, I was explaining to a member of the public group that the room we were next to on the third floor was the maid's room. I couldn't readily think of her name for some reason and stated out loud, "Hmm, what the heck was the maid's name?" The Cell Phone to the Dead called out, "Bridget." I wondered if it was just a coincidence, for I wasn't familiar with the device, but told the person, that the maid's name was Bridget. Next, I heard the word "Sullivan" blurted out in the headphones attached to the cell phone to the dead, and remembered this was the maid's last name. I didn't know what to think. I thought this device might be an interesting tool to experiment with in the future.

Later in the evening, another event happened that I'm not sure I can explain. Unless there was human interaction going on, I don't know how the events played out the way they did. Or, maybe I'm right and Mr. Borden really does hate me. Then again, I don't much care for Mr. Borden either, after all the things I've heard of him. Elizabeth Norwicki is known as the "house psychic" and I'd witnessed the seances she'd performed in the house on a previous investigation. She tries to make Mr. Borden angry, and he shows his anger by shaking a table violently. This night, they took a smaller table into the sitting room, where Mr. Borden was found dead. Five or six of us sat at the table, including myself and Crystal. Elizabeth began by provoking Mr. Borden and bringing up the day of the murder. The table shook, rattled, and rolled as Mr. Borden became more agitated. Elizabeth became distressed, felt ill, and needed to take a moment away to gather herself. When she left the room, I wondered if the table only responded to her. Or if someone else could make it react that way.

I began to provoke Mr. Borden. I tried to make him angry with me, for being a woman and being independent. I didn't think Mr. Borden had a high value for women to begin with, and thought this would tick him off. I kept trying to think of things to say to make Mr. Borden angry with me. I told him that, in these modern times, women didn't have to be under a man's rule any longer. They could work in a man's field and didn't have to listen to any man. That we had the right to vote and could do anything a man could. As I continued on this frame, the table began to respond. Then, before I had a chance to know what was happening, it was attacking me! I held the table back as best I could, but at one point, the exertion was making my arms shake with the strain. I could not see the other side of the table, or make out if any of the other people could be pushing it in any way. Crystal later stated that she could not see everyone from where she was sitting. So I have no way of knowing for sure what exactly happened with that table. I do know one thing, by the time it was over, the table lay in pieces, torn apart by the abuse of whatever force had made it try to attack me that way. I may never know for sure what caused it; I can only guess that I was successful in making Andrew Borden angry.

René sneaks up on Matt Moniz of *Spooky Southcoast* to "ax" him a question. *Courtesy Crystal Washington, WCG*

SUMMING IT UP

Once upon a time, terrible ax murders happened in a home in Fall River. No one can say exactly who the murderer was, or why the murders happened. It does seem to me that the Bordens may still reside there. It also seems as if they have guests in their home that want to stay on with them.

I can say that I am convinced that this house is haunted by more than one spirit, some of whom may be the Bordens, and evidence does suggest that. Adding in the fact that a negative entity may rule the house makes it hard to say for sure what is going on. I think there is more than meets the eye at Lizzie's house, so much more research is needed in this beautiful bed and breakfast.

I also can say that if you want to stay in a house that has paranormal activity and have the chance to investigate it yourself, then Lizzie Borden's Bed & Breakfast is the place for you!

Just don't "ax" the spirits too many questions!

VISITOR INFORMATION

Lizzie Borden's Bed & Breakfast
230 Second Street
Fall River, MA 02721
(508) 675-7333

Tours run from 11 a.m. to 3 p.m.
Rooms are available by reservation.
(Make sure you tell them Whaling City Ghosts sent you!)

CHAPTER FIVE

MY FAVORITE GHOSTS

PRIVATE LOCATIONS

"Family Matters." *Courtesy Crystal Washington, WCG*

The following stories are from locations that wish to remain anonymous, yet have provided me with amazing audio evidence. One thing remains the same: No matter how many cases my team becomes involved with, some of these ghosts reach out and touch our hearts. Aren't we all just souls waiting to be released from our bodies at the moment of death? Will some trauma cause us to be left behind? For me, I hope not, for one thing seems to be the rule with ghosts. They all seem to have a sadness, an anger, or a longing that keeps them locked here in our world. They all seem to want to reach out into the human world.....and touch us!

A HAUNTED LITTLE HOUSE
IN THE DARK WOODS

One of the first private cases that my team became involved with is still one of the most perplexing cases to date. For some reason, there seems to be an intense number of spirits at this home. It's not the house itself, for it's not more than twenty-five years old. But what the problem here may be is the land the house sits on. Another factor, that my Head of Historical Research, Debby, and I have been working on is the contaminants that are present, not only in the river that runs through the property, but in the very ground itself. Could these contaminants, namely Polychlorinated Biphenyls (PCBs), mercury, and cadmium cause a spirit battery that helps to fuel a haunt? We're beginning to think this is a possibility, especially since we've encountered another private home with very similar circumstances. I also think as you read this section and listen to the EVP that accompanies it, you will see how our skill at audio work has grown over the years. Practice makes perfect with paranormal investigation and recovering evidence, as I've said before.

This first case involves the home of some good friends of mine. They had some small amount of activity and had captured a strange photograph in their family room. It was in November of 2005 when I first visited the home to interview one of the owners, Kelly. I brought my recorder and camera and planned to interview her on the activity she had experienced in the home and to find out more about the house she was living in.

Kelly explained to me that she had experienced much more than her husband, Kyle, had. Mostly, what she had experienced had been a couple of "bed shaking" incidents, and, a few times, she had felt like she was being watched. Between having captured one strange picture and the small amount of activity that she had experienced, I wasn't sure that I would capture any evidence. Was I ever wrong!

Kelly explained to me that her home was only about fifteen years old at the time of the occurrences. She also told me about a couple of family members who had recently passed on. One of them had been a suicide. Suicides seem to *stay on*. I'm not sure why—whether it has anything to do with their state of minds when they commit their final acts, or if it is something else. We can only guess at this. The strange dark robed and hooded figure that appeared in the picture Kelly had taken was enough to give anyone chills and I wondered what it had to do with her case. As I researched into the history of the land that the house sat on, I found some interesting facts.

One factor that I think might have something to do with this case is that the house sits on the edge of one side of the Freetown-Fall River State Forest. It also is situated on the edge of a very old part of Dartmouth called Hixville. On a later visit, Kyle took me for a ride around the area, including the place where the family member in question had committed suicide. At one point, driving down a wooded dirt road, we viewed the remains of some of the houses that were burnt down during King Philip's War and were never rebuilt. These empty holes in the ground were a bleak reminder of the violence that once rocked our newborn country.

I had no idea, at the first meeting with Kelly, that all the history that had happened before the house was even built was going to come into play with this case.

After the first initial interview and many investigations, I have come to suspect that the past events that have played out on this land have created many "levels" of hauntings here. Through the years, this particular piece of land has seen it all—from the peaceful Wampanoag hunting and growing things in the area, to the arrival of the "white man." From King Philip's War to the Revolutionary War, all the way into modern times, events have put their mark on this land. During King Philip's War, every house that existed at the time, less than thirty, was burnt to the ground. The empty stone foundations still sit in the woods around this home. They are a constant reminder of how we treated the Wampanoag tribe, the people who existed here before any white man's contributions to the country—the tribe who saved the Pilgrims from starvation. The peaceful tribe that once wandered these lands was almost completely wiped out.

By the end of King Philip's War, the most bloody war per capita that this country has ever seen, only about 400 Wampanoag people existed, and most were sold into slavery. Or executed. Or executed and then drawn and quartered. Talk about barbarianism! Heads of leaders, namely King Philip himself, and Anawan, his war general, were hung outside Fort Plymouth for twenty years! Metacomet's (King Philip) body was never recovered as far as we know, and the belt of the Wampanoag that was surrendered to Benjamin Church was never found. There are stories that it was sent to England, but it remains a mystery as to what happened to this belt, which in its design showed the history of the Wampanoag people.

I have found that these people still remain behind in spirit, and seem forgiving and friendly, considering how they met their ends!

Later, this area was torn once again by the Revolutionary War. Many were still loyal to the King of England, while others wanted freedom from the taxes and rule of the King on the other side of a vast ocean. After that, the Civil War came to tear apart the peace once again. Then, also, there are the lives of farmers and millers, and the many daily dramas that are unknown to us (private family matters) played out every day in history in between the greater events that are recorded. Even Africa has its place in this long and colorful history. At one point, seven black residents petitioned for the right to vote, stating that they'd paid taxes and fought in the Revolutionary War. Later, this area was part of the Underground Railroad, which helped slaves to freedom.

The only reminders of the everyday hardships of the people who planted these fertile lands and walked upon its soil are the family plots that grace the gentle countryside. The only way we can hear them is to listen carefully to the recordings

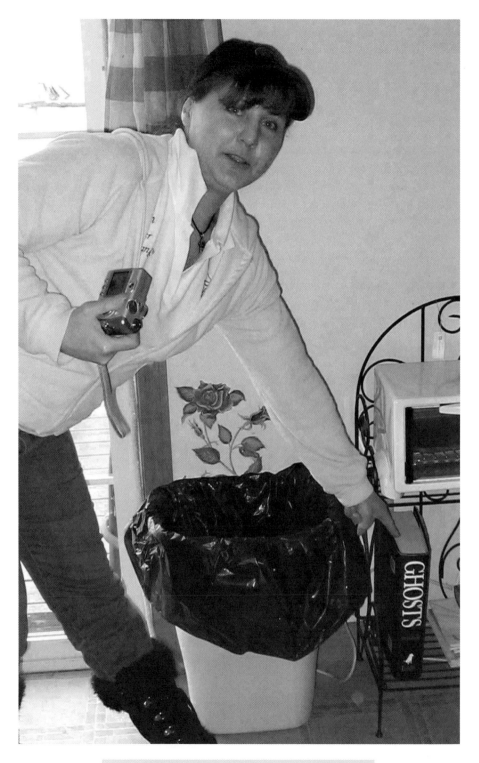

Luann (A. E. Angel) always finds her ghosts! *Courtesy Crystal Washington, WCG*

we gather in these places—then we will hear the voices of people who have lived this history. People who still walk the lands, bodiless, and looking for the things they lost in their lives. People who you are about to hear from, through all the ages in between. For even as we speak of the history of this land that this little house in Dartmouth sits upon, we also have spirits from the modern era.

After my first initial interview with Kelly, I went home thinking I would not find much from my audio. The photographs I'd taken were all negative as to any paranormal evidence. But when I began to go over the audio, I found myself shocked! Almost immediately, I was greeted by the voice of what sounded like a little old lady, saying, *"Hello!"*

 RECORDING

Track 53
[5 Hello]

As I have said before, as you go through these EVPs, you will see that my skill has grown over the years. For these are not as well-edited as the ones you will hear toward the end of this section. I suggest that for the first EVP in this section, you turn up your speakers or headphones and listen carefully; repeat them as needed. I promise that the EVP you will hear at the end will be much easier to hear.

Beginning to think I was mistaken about the level of activity in the house, judging by how quickly I had gotten an EVP, practically within seconds of turning on the recorder, I went on with more enthusiasm.

Kelly and I continued to discuss the home and were also catching up with each other. Soon after this first EVP, a little boy pipes in and declares, *"I want some more applesauce!"*

RECORDING

Track 54
[5 I Want Some More Applesauce]

I have to admit that hearing small children who are apparently spirits, and are dead, really makes my heart ache. I can't help but wonder how it is possible for little children to be left behind in our world. Could it be confusion at being dead? Could they hold onto life more tightly than an adult? I can not even guess, but it always makes me very sad when I come in contact with a child spirit.

Then again, the next EVP makes me wonder just how sad this little boy really is. Isn't whistling a thing you do when you're happy? Or was he just trying to get our attention and let us know he was there? This EVP I call "the whistler" and I believe it may be the same little boy who "wanted more applause." Kelly and I were oblivious to this little tune going on behind us. It only appeared in the audio recording, and I can assure you that neither myself, nor Kelly, had been whistling.

RECORDING

Track 55
[5 Whistler]

Still oblivious to the fact that the spirits had joined us, we continued to chat. Kelly didn't have much to tell me about activity. It seemed as if there wasn't all that much going on in the home. I have come to realize, after five years of investigating this home, that these spirits are not only aware of the living people who reside there, but they are also aware of each other. But as I said, I did not expect to find much in the recordings. As I've investigated this home many times, I've found that the activity seems to be cautious, as if these spirits are respectful of the homeowners.

Kelly had explained to me about a friend and a family member who had recently left this life behind. One had died of illness, the other had taken his own life. As she explained the circumstances of their deaths, another strange EVP pipes in.

This EVP actually has two voices in it. The first, I think may be a child, but I can't be sure, for the second EVP takes over the smaller voice, saying, *"Anybody else die?"*

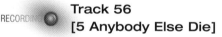

RECORDING

Track 56
[5 Anybody Else Die]

It seemed an odd thing to ask. But then again, we were speaking of the recently deceased. My only explanation is that this spirit was fully aware of what we were talking about.

The next EVP brings back the era in which the Wampanoag once roamed these lands. Kelly and I came to sit in the sumptuous and beautiful family room. The sun shone in the ceiling-high windows and made the atmosphere seem to be one in which the dead should not be wandering. An atmosphere in which 300-year-old dead people should not be speaking. *"Attuckquock,"* (ah-tewk-qwok) a Wampanoag word which means male deer, is very appropriate in this home.

RECORDING

Track 57
[5 Attuckquock]

Trophy bucks adorn the walls, as Kyle, the husband of the home, is an avid hunter. At the same time, a later EVP recorded at the home makes me wonder if this word was actually meant as a name. The unfortunate part about this EVP is the fact that when I first began investigating this home, I did not have the audio equipment that I do now. It was only recently when I went over this audio again that I recovered this EVP. I did get a chance to hear from this Wampanoag spirit again, but that comes later.

The last EVP from this unofficial interview at the home surprised me very much! Not only are these aware spirits that understand what we're talking about, but they also must realize that they are dead! I was drawing the interview to a close and preparing to leave. I was also explaining to Kelly that sometimes spirits attach to people rather than places. At the time, I wasn't completely sure that I would recover any evidence. If I did recover any evidence, I wasn't quite sure what the "source" of the haunt was, for I hadn't done the research on the history of the area. I had told Kelly that it was very possible that one or more spirits could possibly be attached to either herself or her husband. As Kelly and I bring the session to an end, a voice comes through: *"I'm that spirit...Luann!"*

RECORDING ● **Track 58**
[5 I'm That Spirit Luann]

The pronunciation of my name is a bit strange to me, but I have heard many people of differing nationalities pronounce my name in various ways. I don't have a very common name, and many living people don't know how to pronounce it. I'm sure I can understand a spirit of an unknown era having difficulty in that respect. Either way, I was at once captured and fascinated by the audio that I had never dreamed I would record in this home! It was enough to begin a series of official investigations there.

Over the next few years, I did return to investigate again. The investigations produced some great audio recordings. I came closer to the spirits of this house than I knew was possible—especially considering the vast number of spirits that seem to be present and accounted for here. I recorded what sounded to me like Wampanoag war cries, possible cult chants were captured with the haunting word, "Hemotep," being repeated in a hoarse whisper. The name "Tobias" rang out into our world in a voice very similar to our "attuckquock" EVP that was recorded on my first visit to this home. I heard the name, "Adam," for the very first time. Little girls called out a greeting in almost a chorus of voices, "Hello Luann....Hello Luann... Hello Luann," each voice different and distinct. I was amazed! Unfortunately, these EVP may have to be recovered at a later date if it is possible, for the computer that I'd been using for audio editing decided to pick up and die one day. I can only hope that it will be possible to pull them off the hard drive that I saved out of that poor haunted, over-worked computer!

Noticing some interesting similarities between two properties I'd investigated, I decided it was time to re-visit this house on the edge of the woods. In November of 2010, I did just that, and once again, I sat in this beautiful, well-kept home, to interview, alone, with Kelly. I set up my recorder in my favorite room for audio. It was a big sunny family room with a high ceiling that seemed to bring about very clear EVP. I whispered to Adam that this was his home and that he should stay here. I can only hope that he has either decided to stay on where he came from, or that he has "crossed over" to the other side since my last recording of him.

Kelly and I hadn't seen each other socially for some months, so we sat comfortably in the living room and caught up. After a bit of socializing, I began to ask how things had been on the paranormal front. Once again, she didn't have all that much outright activity to report. One thing that did concern her was the fact that her dog, an older and sweet beagle, seemed to have times when she seemed uncomfortable in the house. She would also yelp and appeared to be looking at something when nothing was there. She would stare off into space and seem to be watching something unseen to human eyes move about the room. I took note of what Kelly told me, and, as we spoke, the digital recorder that I love best was rolling, listening more closely than our ears could for signs of the other side.

After interviewing Kelly for about an hour, I set up a date for our investigation and brought my recorder home with excitement. Once again, as I did my review, I was blown away by the ghostly drama that was invisible to our eyes. It was also the first time I had the pleasure of meeting "Dick!" Along with Dick, it seemed as if many of the original spirits were still present and they seemed just as happy to interact with the living as they had in the past! I think you'll understand later in this section why it is that I carry a secret smile as I introduce you to our new spirit, Dick. For now, just remember I am once again pleased to find a responsive atmosphere where the spirits seem to be purposely allowing their voices to be recorded. You will know why I smile and laugh as I go over this audio, hearing the enthusiastic replies of the spirits when they greet Kelly at the end of our interview session.

Once again, as I reviewed the evidence, I found the spirits quite happy to speak, though there were some that I have not included, due to the fact that they were soft and there was interference from a humidifier in the garage. The garage was directly below the room the recorder was in. Unknown to me, at times, it caused a hum in my recording. Even so, the voices of the dead could be heard ringing through the family room.

After two soft calls of "*baby*," what I think may be the same female voice states, "*I will go.*" (Not included.) She did not sound like the same woman from earlier recordings to my ear. I wondered if she could be a new spirit, or if she had been there all along and just hadn't spoken up until then.

Kelly and I sat comfortably in front of the fireplace and, in the other room, the recorder kept rolling. Once again, we hadn't seen each other for some weeks, and were enjoying catching up, more than investigating. But that didn't matter. The spirits had something to say! I was later to find that the spirit in this next EVP was referring to me specifically. In this audio clip you can hear the hum of the humidifier, which without my knowledge, must have switched on downstairs in the garage. I could not hear this audibly, but the recorder certainly did. Also, in the background, Kelly's voice can be heard. "*Get the f--- out,*" is almost exactly in the center of this clip. The loop that you will hear should bring it out more clearly for you.

Track 59
[5 Get The F Out]

Shortly after, "*Get out,*" can be heard. (Not included.) I was beginning to think these were new spirits attracted to an energy source or some other undefinable cause. I'd never been unwelcome by the spirits in this home before. I hate to admit it, but I was a little hurt by these responses. However, it wasn't enough to stop me from being excited at the rest of the audio I'd recovered this day!

Cold November sunshine lit the room as Kelly and I continued to chat amiably. The humidifier continued its hum in the garage, as a male voice, a definite Class A recording broke the stillness of the family room. "*Dick!*"

Track 60
[5 Dick]

Later, once I'd finished reviewing the audio for this day, I asked Kyle and Kelly if the name Dick meant anything to either of them. I knew that Kyle's father had passed on around this time last year, so I thought maybe this could have been his name. But that was not his first name, so I was left with the mystery of just who Dick was, and where he had come from.

I was nearing the end of the recording, pondering if I would hear responses from any of the children I had heard during earlier investigations and interviews with Kelly. When I had all but given up, I finally heard a child's voice. A faint little voice saying, "Mommy home." (EVP not included.)

Encouraged that at least some of the spirits still seemed to be friendly, I went on and was not disappointed when I recovered an almost answering EVP to "Mommy's home." It seems to be a slightly stronger voice, and I believe, a different voice from the first. I can't be sure, but I think this second voice is questioning the first as to where "mommy" is. "*Where's mommy?*" only makes me want to know more about the origins of these child spirits. Had they lost their mother somehow? Or had death taken her away from them?

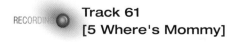

Track 61
[5 Where's Mommy]

My biggest surprise as to just how responsive these spirits are to the living came at the very end of the recording. I can actually say that when I clipped these next two EVPs, they brought a smile to my face! We ventured back into the family room to recover the recorder and end our session together. Kelly told me a few more details; then, turning toward the recorder, she said, "Any of you that want to come and say hello," she pauses, and an EVP pipes in, "Hello!" (Not included. This EVP was too hard to clip out and retain clarity, so I have left it out.) Kelly goes on, "...you're more than welcome." The EVP is so bright and cheery, I couldn't help but laugh aloud to hear it. It said: *"I say HI! to Kelly."*

RECORDING **Track 62**
[5 I say HI to Kelly]

This shows me an aware spirit that knows who is speaking and exactly what that person is saying, then responds immediately with what I think is good intention. I found that as much as I thought I knew what to expect from this house, that, as always, when dealing with the paranormal, I never knew what to expect!

My team was looking forward to returning for an official investigation. They had heard a lot about this house, and all of its ghosts, for quite some time. I was excited to see how having Tara, our Team Psychic, on the case would turn out. It worked out much better than I had imagined it could!

I also found out that Dick, our new spirit at the house, wasn't exactly happy to see me return. This surprised me quite a bit because, for as long as I can remember, spirits seemed to want to communicate with me—and even learn my name and call for me specifically. I wondered, as I went over the audio from this investigation, if I'd done something to offend Dick. But I don't think I was the problem, in this case; I think it may be Dick who really had the issue. My team and I, unfortunately, represent the fact that Dick is dead. I hope on further investigations that I can get to the bottom of what Dick's problem really is.

The first EVP from this investigation came as a surprise, once again. It made it apparent that the other spirits in the house were also aware of Dick. *"You're not supposed to be down here....Dick sent you along!"*

RECORDING **Track 63**
[5 Not Down Here Dick Sent You Along]

You'll hear my voice, in the forefront, telling Kelly and Kyle that I had eaten, "...before I came....my crazy day!" The EVP wraps around my own voice, speaking when I pause, as if he wants to make sure I hear. It also brought to memory that deep voice that rang through the family room declaring his identity, *"Dick,"* during my last visit. He, apparently, had contact with the other spirits who visited the house, but why was it that Dick seemed so disagreeable? So very offended that my team and I were there? Or was it just specifically me that Dick had a problem with?

As I continued to listen to the audio from the investigation, I saw again how valuable a team psychic really could be. Tara had been sitting in her "circle" and trying to encourage the spirits to come and communicate with her. She explained that she didn't usually hear words, but that it was more like she saw pictures in her head, or felt things. She was describing a young boy she saw of about 8-9 years of age who wore shorter pants. I supplied her with the word *britches*, and she said she thought that might be right.

Kyle, who was in the room, asks, "What's the boy's name?" A small, high voice answers, very quickly, softly, "Michael." Just after this you hear Tara answer, "My first instinct's Michael." (Not included.) Tara continued on, saying that the boy, Michael, had shown her the year 1891 and that it was important to him somehow. She wasn't sure if that was the year he died or if it had some other significance.

Not long after this clip, Tara was trying to make sense of what she was seeing. Her sentence was disjointed and didn't make much sense until the end. She said something close to, "It's not like....It doesn't....Like you said....I don't..." Then at the end of this jumble, she says, "You usually have people in the church talking." This, to her, meant that most of the "good gossip" came from the churchgoers, and that the churches also kept records of everything going on in the community. During the disjointed sentence, a female voice said, "That's Michael." (Not Included.) I'm not sure if she was pointing out to us that it was Michael who had just spoken to us—that maybe he was the boy Tara was describing—or if she meant something else. No matter what she meant, it was amazing to see one spirit being aware of another spirit. At the same time, it was even more amazing because they all seemed to be aware of each other in this home!

Shortly after this, Tara asked if I would start an EVP session and ask questions having to do with what I'd learned of these spirits in the past. She was hoping that by having me remind them of things to do with their lives, it might help her to communicate better with them. Thinking hard about the evidence I'd recovered in the past, I pointed to one of the trophy bucks hanging on the wall, and asked, "Is that an attuckquock?" The answer received surprised me and made me wonder if "attuckquock" could also be a name, and not just the word for "male deer." In this clip, you will hear my voice asking if the buck was an attuckquock; then at the very end of the clip, you'll hear a soft whisper, "I am!" (Not included.) This begged the question about whether the word *attuckquock* was meant as the name of this man, or if the spirit was simply pointing out the male deer on the wall. Maybe he felt a kinship for Kyle, since Kyle enjoyed hunting. Maybe this unknown Native man was a hunter, too. I have been searching for a Wampanoag man named "Attuckquock," and, so far, I have not found anyone in history with this name. But almost all of the history of the Wampanoag came before the white man arrived, so very little is known of these very spiritual people. I can only say, for now, that I will listen for this distinctive male voice in the future, and hope that he can clarify his identity for me!

I've never thought that ghosts could eat, but at the same time, some of them have asked for food, like our little friend who has a fetish for apple sauce. This next EVP shows that some spirits understand that they no longer own a body, and in turn, a stomach. We had finished our EVP session by this time. René had wandered over and taken a cookie out of the bag she had brought to help encourage the children to come closer. I asked her to, "Hand up that bag, I'll open it up and give them cookies!" Directly after this declaration, a soft whisper lets us know, that he, *"Can't eat nothing...nothing!"*

 RECORDING **Track 64**
[5 Can't Eat Nothing Nothing]

Not long after this, the spirits once again show how aware they are of each other. Our friend, the beagle, was clicking and clacking her way across the hardwood floors, and I spoke to her, petting and scratching her. I asked her if she was a good girl, and told her she was a good girl. During my brief petting session, a male voice comes in and says, *"God Dick....get out!"*

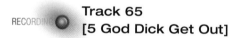 RECORDING **Track 65**
[5 God Dick Get Out]

Was Dick so abusive that it applied to the other spirits there and they wish him gone? Did he somehow become "alpha" spirit in the house and the others do not appreciate his reign? I have to say, I can't understand why Dick has it in for me, nor can I understand how all the other spirits are being affected by his attitude.

Noticing that their beagle seemed to be uncomfortable, I asked Kelly about it. She told me that her dog did this a lot, and that many times she seemed to be looking at something that wasn't visible to human eyes. The poor dog wandered around, looking from place to place and didn't seem as if she could settle down. I mentioned that the dog seemed to be unsettled and Kelly said that she'd been like that. I ask, "Has she?" Immediately after this, a spirit states, *"I'm right here!"*

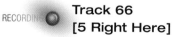 RECORDING **Track 66**
[5 Right Here]

You hear the clacking of dog claws on the floor and I say, "It's like she doesn't know what to do with herself." Then at the very end, you hear what appears to be two separate voices say, "*Bubble...bubble.*" I mused about that possibly being what they called the dog, for her name was not bubble; but who knows what the ghosts may think of her? I did not include a loop for this, but you can hear it if you listen to the original file carefully—it's at the very end.

Now, the next EVP made me consider whether it was directed specifically at me. After all, someone was telling me to "get out" during our interview only a week before this investigation. Tara seems to think that these spirits liked to watch what was going on in and around the home. For some reason, the spirits showed her groundhogs, and she asked the homeowners if they had groundhogs around. Tara thanks Kelly for answering, "Yes," to her question, for it seemed an odd sort of thing for her to ask. Just after she says "thank you," a spirit whispers, "I hate you!" (Not included.) I have to admit, my feelings were a little hurt by this EVP. I'm not used to being hated—by the living, *or* the dead!

The next EVP shows that the child spirits of the home are still present. I also think it shows that they are aware, for the question they ask, I think, refers to the newer members of the team whom they have not met yet, namely René and Tara. Tara had heard a word in her head, and she was describing this. She said she heard the word, "sanctuary" and Kyle then said, "That's....that's weird, huh?" He goes on to say something else, but the EVP comes up over his voice, making it hard to understand his words. The EVP is much easier to understand, "*Who are you?*"

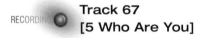

Track 67
[5 Who Are You]

Tara goes on to say that she feels like things should be moving in here. I had seen some physical manipulation of objects in the house, so I kept quiet, watching to see if they would show her their ability to move things. Nothing moved and the investigation went on.

The next EVP made me wonder if there were also African influences in the area at one time. As mentioned earlier, I had found that Dartmouth had freed slaves who had demanded voting rights. They stated that they'd paid taxes, had fought in the Revolutionary War, and wanted more rights. There was also a black cemetery in the town, but no one knew its location. Many think that buildings went up right overtop it. Tara continued to go on about how she believed that if things could fly, they would. She also states that if the homeowners wanted that (flying objects), it could happen. Of course, Kelly doesn't want that, as she states in this clip. As they are speaking, a whisper, which sounds female to me, says, "*Kersa.*"

Track 68
[5 Kersa]

Gabby checks EMF levels in a private home. *Courtesy Crystal Washington, WCG*

In researching the name *Kersa*, I have found two references. One is an area in Ethiopia which lies along the Kersa River. Second, it is possibly a name, and seems to mean politeness and having good manners. I'm hoping that I can find a better reference as to what exactly this spirit means by the word, be it a name or a place. The Portuguese also have a word that sounds just like this word, meaning "thing." Either way, I've taken to calling this young, female spirit, "Kersa."

Now, I'm not sure if Tara could "hear" these words, or if something was shown to her, but she thought it would be okay if we "woke up" the kids. I asked her if she was sure, for I'd never tried anything like that before with them. Usually, during the day, the children were more active than they were at night. I have speculated on why this was the case. I've only come up with two ideas. Either they believe that it's time for bed at night and settle down, or they are afraid of the dark and find a place to hide until daylight comes again. After being assured by Tara that it would be all right to wake up the children, I started calling out to them. I've always liked the child spirits there; they seemed to be enthusiastic about my visits and usually called me by name to say hello.

"Kids!" I call out; then, at the end of the recording I call, "Come on out!" But in between these two phrases, a man's voice tells me I'm, "*Being a b---- about it!*"

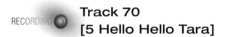

RECORDING **Track 69**
[5 Being a Btch About It]

I am left thinking that this must be my friend, Dick, though I can't say that I was being mean about anything. I have had many experiences with the child spirits in this house, and if anything, my heart goes out to them. I was trying to treat them gently, but I guess Dick didn't agree!

I believe this next set of EVP shows just how aware and responsive these children are. One little girl spirit seems to be mimicking and repeating after me. Tara had been looking over a map of the area around the home and noting that many prominent names were listed as residents. She talks about some of these names, and at the same time mentions that she was born up north. I randomly call out, "Say hello!" A female child's voice answers back, "*Hello!*" Tara goes on to say she was born in "North Andover," then says that a lot of the surnames are up there (used in the area where she was born). At the same time, I call out, "Say hello, Tara!" That same female child answers, "*Hello Tara!*"

RECORDING **Track 70**
[5 Hello Hello Tara]

I have to admit that in all my time investigating haunts, I've never had a spirit respond so enthusiastically! This little child didn't seem to mind that I had woken her up! And she didn't call me names. But in the end, it seems Dick was ticked off at the fact that, either, I had woken up the children, or he was mad at the child for responding to me.

In this next clip, you hear Kyle saying that, "...you just have to be going," but he doesn't finish this sentence. Then Tara explains, "The child... that one... that's what freaked me out." In the background, over Tara's voice, you can hear the same female spirit that had repeated my words in the previous EVP say, "I'll be at the (something unintelligible—may be the word "store")," but the last word is cut out by a male voice that says, "Let's go!"

RECORDING **Track 71**
[5 I'll Be At The Let's Go]

Once again, I have to ask if this is our friend, Dick. It seems to me that he thinks he is the ruler of the house and has the authority to order the other spirits. Some of the spirits don't seem all that happy about this arrangement, as in the EVP, "God Dick, get out!" I am still left puzzled as to how so many spirits seem to gravitate to this home, who is this spirit Dick, and why does he seem to dislike me so much?

I have decided that, as soon as I can, I'm going to go back to this house and try to have a heart-to-heart talk with Dick. I think he may be offended by the fact that I ask many questions of the spirits. Maybe he thinks I'm going to pry into his afterlife, or demand that he "cross over" to the other side. Possibly he's threatened by me, for I represent the fact that he is no longer living.

I can assure him that if he doesn't want to respond to me or my team, he doesn't have to. I will never force him to do anything that he doesn't want to do. But I will also assure him that if he ever changes his mind and decides that he wants to communicate with us, we will always be there for him. All he has to do is speak up. In my eyes, only time will tell if Dick can learn to trust the living. As for me, I'll be waiting for that day!

THE HAUNTED MILL

During the late nineteenth century to the early twentieth century, the area known as southeastern Massachusetts was made prosperous by textile mills. These mills were rampant with unsafe working conditions and child labor. Many of the mills depended on the rivers for power and were close by the water sources of the New Bedford/Fall River area. They also spilled many of their chemicals into these waters. As you know, my team has been working on the effects of these chemicals on our haunts. We still ask: Does the fact that these chemicals must still exist, to some extent, around the mills help to fuel the haunts? Whaling City Ghosts was lucky enough to investigate one of these ancient mills in the city of Fall River. The evidence we recovered was more than any of us expected.

Our first visit to this mill building was in January of 2006. Gabby Lawson ran video, while Crystal Washington ran audio, EMF, temperature readings, and a still camera. As usual, I carried my trusty Canon and ran audio for the duration of the night. Almost immediately, I began to record some shocking EVP. As we spoke with the other team that had joined us for the evening, we were oblivious to the blood-curdling screams that went on behind us, often drowning out our voices. I am not positive, but it seems as if one spirit was very upset about us being in the building. The screams that take over the audio are quite loud, so loud, in fact, that I had to bring the sound level down to remove the distortion of the screams. Yet we were unaware of them at the time. The screams seem high enough to be female, while the words, "*Who are you?*" and "*Leave!*" seem to be male. When I listen to the screams, I can almost make out the words, "get out" embedded in them, but can not be sure. One thing I do know is that this spirit was very distressed that we were in the building.

Track 72
[5 Screamer]
 RECORDING **(I have looped the words at the end, rather than the screams, which I find disturbing to listen to.)**

As we discussed the set up of equipment and where we would like to begin EVP sessions, we had no idea that someone wasn't pleased to have us invade their building. I couldn't help but ponder those screams. Did they have anything to do with a horrible mill fire that happened close to this building where some of the mill workers had perished? Or was it the building this spirit was feeling territorial about? Recently, we found out more that made us believe we knew the identity of not only the woman screaming, but the man speaking.

Sarah Cornell was a mill worker who had traveled quite a lot seeking employment during her lifetime. Born on May 3, 1802, she'd seen Connecticut, Massachusetts, and New Hampshire in her thirty years on earth. Maybe it had been a mistake for her to return to Massachusetts for mill work. Coming back to Fall River, she again met a man she'd known before, in Connecticut. Ephraim K. Avery had been the minister in a church she'd attended. Later, in Fall River, Minister Avery offered Sarah some help. Apparently, there were letters in the church accusing her of fornication and other behaviors that were frowned upon at the time. Sarah wanted to turn over a new leaf, but it appears that the minister wanted more than to help this poor mill girl. Sarah would be allowed to be a member of the church the minister was affiliated with, and he would destroy the letters kept in the church's records, if she would sleep with him.

On December 20, 1832, Sarah Cornell was found hanging from a stackpole in what was then the Durfee Farm, and is now present-day Kennedy Park. It was assumed she had committed suicide. Shortly after her burial, some interesting evidence was found—a letter found in Sarah's belongings that stated if anything happened to her, to inquire of the Minister Avery. There was also other correspondence between herself and the minister, which gave cause to exhume her body, or "disinter" it, as it states in her autopsy report. What they found made it apparent she had not committed suicide, but had been murdered. What causes me to believe that the screams from this EVP are Sarah Cornell and the words at the end may be Minister Avery, as he murdered her and dragged her to the place he left her hanging, includes a variety of facts.

Loosing Whaling City Ghosts' very own history bloodhound, Debby White-Paiva, on the case brought about the discovery of many facts relating to Sarah's murder. She not only found the historical documents pertaining to the case, but also a book written by one of the ladies who had prepared Sarah's body for burial, Catherine R. (Reed) Williams. In her account, Catherine notes many injuries, describing them carefully. A rope had embedded itself in Sarah's neck, a half an inch deep. The skin on the backs of her legs had been scraped off as if she'd been dragged some distance. Her knees were also skinned in this manner and had bruises and grass stains on them. Bruises shaped like hands with fingers in the back and thumbs to the front marked both of her hips. One of her arms was bent so the hand stuck up. When the ladies tried to straighten her limb, it snapped into place as if it had been broken. More was revealed when the letters were found, and it was decided, a little over a month after her burial, to disinter her body. During the autopsy, it was discovered that someone had tried to remove a four-month old fetus from Sarah's womb.

Sarah had been buried with a broken piece of a beautiful comb in her hair. It had been one of her most-prized possessions. Shortly before her death, she had brought it to a jeweler to be repaired. Pieces of this comb were found between the mill buildings and the Durfee farm where her body had been found hanging.

It was decided her death had been ruled a suicide quite hastily. Other evidence at the scene should have pointed to foul play. I'm left to believe that if, due to the times, that the men involved had been afraid to examine this woman's body too closely. The way Sarah's body had been found made it next to impossible that she had hung herself to death in this way. Her knees had only been four inches above the ground; she could easily have stood up. A handkerchief found next to her body was bunched up and later found to be soaked with saliva. The knot used to tie the rope about her neck was not a hangman's knot, or even a slip knot, but a "clove-hitch" knot, which in order to tighten, two hands are needed, one on each side to pull. So in effect, someone had pulled those two ends and strangled Sarah before they ever hung her. Witnesses reported hearing a "woman in distress" as early as

7:30 p.m. when Ellinor Owen reported screeching in her home, about a quarter of a mile away from the mill. William Hamilton reported the groans of a female around 8:45 p.m. By the bits of broken hair comb, the reports of screaming and groans, the damage done to Sarah's person makes me believe that whoever killed Sarah didn't only drag her all the way to her death. Sarah's murderer tortured and abused her, tried to remove her baby from her, and possibly raped her, before he finally strangled her to death. He then, haphazardly, left her hanging on the Durfee farm. I can't imagine poor Sarah's terror during these acts committed against her. Now that I know her, I can never forget her.

Testimony in the case points to Minister Avery. The letters going back and forth between Sarah and the minister plan a meeting on the eighteenth of December, and if it was "too stormy," then to meet on the twentieth. In the last letter from Avery to Sarah, she is asked to meet him before the mills have closed for the day. The machinery running in the mills would have muffled any sounds of her screams. When people in their houses began to notice, did he stuff his handkerchief in her mouth to quiet her?

Sarah's doctor had interesting testimony when he was brought to the witness stand. It seems the minister had given Sarah some poison. She stated that the minister had told her if she took thirty drops of the poison, it would rid her of the baby. The doctor had then told Sarah that four or five drops would have been fatal to not only the baby, but her as well. With all the letters, the testimony of witnesses called from out of state, the physical abuse on Sarah's body, Minister Avery was found not guilty and released.

It seems that the public, those who had heard about it—even those from afar who had read accounts of the case in newspapers—knew the truth, though. Minister Avery barely escaped being lynched in Fall River, Massachusetts, the site of the murders, and again in New Hampshire, where he had moved, hoping to escape his ill-gotten fame.

Is that Sarah we hear screaming in this audio recording? Is it Minister Avery asking who we are, and telling us to leave? In effect, to mind our own business? I can't say for sure, but I have a feeling, deep in my heart that these horrible, blood-curdling screams are those of Sarah Cornell, a poor mill girl, murdered at such a young age. Her only crime, getting pregnant by the wrong man. I hope to bring her memory some justice, to ease her broken soul. For there was a time when people from all over the country came to Sarah's humble stone, set upon the Durfee farm, where her battered and abused body had been found. I can only hope the words set upon that stone can bring her memory, her ghost, her spirit, some peace. For you, for myself, for my team, I wish for us to remember Sarah well.

Sarah Maria Cornell
May 3, 1802-December 20, 1832
"And here thou maketh thy lonely bed,

Thou poor forlorn and injured one,
Here rest thy aching head."

The next clip you are about to hear is one of the creepiest voices that I've ever heard in an EVP. Earlier in the day, Gabby and I had visited the mill building to give it a once-over and see how difficult it would be for us to set up equipment. It seems as if this spirit recognized us from our visit. He greets us as we settled ourselves down in a long corridor that we thought would be a good area to record video and audio. *"Hello again,"* is said in a scratchy and quite creepy male voice.

 Track 73
[5 Hello Again]

n being able to recognize us and greet us in such a manner makes me believe that these are aware spirits who can take in their environment and react to it.

Making ourselves comfortable in the long corridor, we began an EVP session, unaware of the creepy greeting we'd received. We took turns asking questions that related to the mill era, hoping that we would hit upon the right questions to gain a response from the other side. Now, as I mentioned earlier, these mill buildings were rampant for unsafe working conditions. This next clip makes me wonder, just what exactly had happened to this poor spirit who seemed as if he may have been the victim of some industrial accident. *"My eyes,"* is said in a very strong whisper.

 **Track 74**
[5 My Eyes]

Listen carefully; there is almost a ringing, or tinkling sound, that distorts the words a bit. Was he so close to the recorder that he distorts the sound, or is it some sound artifact caused by his voice ringing through different dimensions? Did he become blinded while working? On the other side of life, do spirits experience the failings of the human body? Was this poor spirit still feeling the pain of whatever injury had inflicted him?

We had been in the corridor for about an hour when we decided that we would move down to the lower level of the building and begin another EVP session there. As Gabby and Crystal walked away from me, I felt overwhelmed by a strong tingling feeling, and I swore that I heard a whisper behind me. I turned to look toward the end of the hallway, but did not see anything visibly. Taking a chance, I grabbed a couple camera shots of the end of the hall. Gabby and Crystal stopped to look back at me and asked if I was going to join them downstairs. I hurried to catch up, but as I reviewed the pictures I had just taken, I discovered that there had been someone at the end of the hallway after all.

A small, child-sized dark-colored apparition had shown up in the pictures, though it had not been visible with the naked eye. In one shot, it looks as if the shape was walking out into the hallway opening, its arms seem to be swinging as they would with the motion of walking. In the next, its arm was raised as if waving at me. These two pictures are some of the best apparition pictures I've ever caught while on investigation.

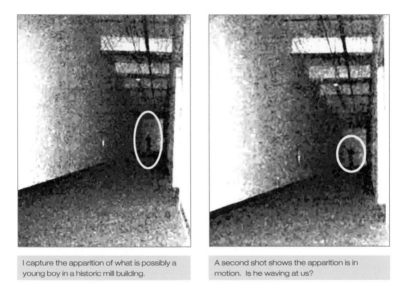

I capture the apparition of what is possibly a young boy in a historic mill building.

A second shot shows the apparition is in motion. Is he waving at us?

I stopped for a moment to show the girls what I had captured, and unbeknownst to me, I captured another EVP. Was *"Nathaniel Hall"* the name of the spirit that I captured with my camera?

RECORDING

Track 75
[5 Nathaniel Hall]

To this day, I cannot find this name relating to the mill building. Could he have been an orphan taken in to work at the mill in exchange for a daily meal or two? I may never know, but I will never forget Nathaniel Hall. Or the way he seemed to want my attention and had actually waved at me!

After this initial investigation at the mill, we were intrigued with the evidence recovered. Visiting the owners of the building, we reviewed the evidence with them. They were just as fascinated as we were. Later in the year, we were allowed to return to investigate once again. The owners were interested in the spirits that resided in their historic building, but were afraid of what publicity would do for their security situation. They did not want to have to employ overnight security guards and asked that we keep the location as private as possible. We gladly agreed and looked forward to working with them to preserve the secrecy of the building and its invisible residents.

We decided to start in the attic, since we had not had much of a chance to visit there on our first investigation. We found it oppressive and stuffy—and that we were not all that welcome there. As we wandered about, exclaiming over the antique machinery that was left abandoned, a voice told us, "Get out!" (Not included.) Though we were oblivious to this warning to leave the attic, we didn't stay long anyway. It was extremely hot and dusty and mummified pigeons and pigeon droppings lined the floor, so we returned to the lower levels. We were hoping that if we spent more time in the hallway where I had captured the apparition pictures, that we might gain some more evidence. At the least, we were hoping to capture EVP evidence of this spirit.

Just before we decided to head out of the attic, we recorded one more EVP there. As we moved toward the stairs, anxious to find a cooler spot, a scream, and then, "*It burns*," can be heard just before I say that we don't want to spend too much time up here. (Not included.) Without knowing we had just recorded another EVP, one that may have had to do with the previous EVP about someone's eyes, we moved carefully back to the stairs. Even as we did, we marveled over the taste of history that we felt in the attic. This building was closer to what it had been in the past and the old remains of machinery reminded onlookers of what the building used to be like in its hay days. We couldn't help but imagine what it had been like to work there during the summer. Small windows lined the sides of the rooms, not much ventilation for a room that must have risen to hellish temperatures during the summer with multiple machines running.

Once again we got ourselves as comfortable as we could in the long hallway where we'd caught the pictures of the apparition that had appeared on our first investigation. Hoping that the apparition would show itself again, I kept taking still shots, while Gabby kept up her vigilant video recording. The apparition did not appear, however; but we did get an EVP that again proved that these spirits were aware.

As we were getting ready to go down to the first floor to do more investigating, a voice called out my name, "Luann." (Not included.) Not realizing we had an intelligent spirit speaking with us, we returned to the first-floor room near the bathrooms to do a bit more audio and video work.

The temperature difference between the first floor and the attic was like comparing heaven and hell. We gladly sat down upon the cool floor and took turns asking questions of the spirits we knew to be there. We sat quietly, thinking of questions that might encourage the spirits of the mill workers who had once graced this building with their living bodies, to work and toil, and sometimes die in this mill. Some time passed before we recorded another EVP that involved a full name. "*Raymond Lopes*." Again, we have not been able to find this name, except in modern times.

RECORDING

Track 76
[5 Raymond Lopes]

Our researcher, Debby, may be able to find this soul at some later date. I do have to admit that it is very frustrating when having a full name and still not being able to place the spirit. We hope that someday we will know who the spirits of the mill building were in life. Though I can't shake his hand and tell him that it was nice to meet him, I can wish that he, and the other spirits here can find peace. As long as I live, I can never forget those blood curdling screams that rang through the building without our knowledge. Now that I understand Sarah's torment associated with those chilling notes, they are even more disturbing. I will always hope that these spirits who endured the conditions of this building on hot summer days and freezing winters can break the chains of life that bind them here, and move on to a happier place. For Sarah to know peace and Avery to only know divine justice.

A "WICKED" HAUNTED HOUSE IN ACUSHNET

This next house I will bring you to visit is a private residence in the town of Acushnet, in southeastern Massachusetts. It is said to have been standing before the days of the Revolutionary War. It sits along the Acushnet River, a river polluted with mercury and PCBs from the days of the mill era. This particular home was very hard to trace. It was originally part of "Olde Dartmouth" which consisted of New Bedford, Dartmouth, Fairhaven, and Acushnet. In over 300 years, the town lines changed four times.

One thing remains constant. This house is extremely haunted. There is even a rumor that one of the former homeowners was having a mental breakdown due to the ghosts. Additionally, there is a record that the Quakers held a meeting about the paranormal activity in the town of Acushnet. This house has been a home, and, at one time, a funeral parlor, run by one family who owned it. The back door, where bodies were taken into the funeral parlor, still exists. There is even a story that a man, who had fallen off the mast of a whaling ship, fell, breaking his neck and was presumed dead. When he got to the funeral parlor in this home, he awoke, only to be smothered by the mortician. If he had truly broken his neck, then maybe he was better off. Medicine wasn't what it is today, and I'm sure the prognosis for a person with a broken neck was not very good back then!

This home has seen so much history over the years, that it's easy to think that it may be haunted. But why so many ghosts? Why are they so aware and responsive? Once again, I think that this home has the possibility of having a "spirit battery" in the form of contaminants which have been dumped into the river which runs nearby. It is because of this home, and the one in Dartmouth that made me believe in such a possibility.

Whaling City Ghosts' partner, Starborn Support, had investigated this home prior to our investigation, along with good friends Andrew Lake of Greenville Paranormal and Matt Moniz, Independent Investigator and Science Adviser to *Spooky Southcoast*. So far, all of them have reported that they have had personal experiences here and recorded both audio and video of the activity that occurs in this house. I couldn't wait to investigate here myself, and was looking forward to our first visit.

The home seems to have an element of mystery to it, for how can one house be so haunted? And how can it have so many ghosts who apparently span a good deal of history occurring in the area? There are spirits from those aware of not only the investigators, but of each other; spirits that warn the others not to speak, for the investigators are listening; to doors that open on their own captured on video by Andrew Lake. This house is a hotbed of paranormal activity!

On closer inspection, it looks just like any other historic home in the area. Built in the New England tradition, made to last and face the harsh weather conditions that the region is famous for. Once inside, you'll meet the wonderful family who occupies it, and the ghosts who seem to call it home, too.

On July 16, 2010, Whaling City Ghosts and Eric LaVoie of DART (Dartmouth Anomalies Research Team) joined together to investigate the home. I had worked with Eric on cases in the past and had found him not only to be a great investigator, but a wonderful person who is a pleasure to work with. I've taken to calling him my "para-brother from another mother" for we've become fast friends through the medium of paranormal investigation. He was very excited to join my team once again and brought video equipment to supplement our equipment.

We began the night by setting up our cameras and recorders, and helping Eric set up his. We made sure to cover the hot spots that had been reported by other investigators who have investigated this house. We took Renés advice during set up. She had been here previously with Starborn Support. Unfortunately, we did not capture anything with the video cameras. But we sure did record some interesting EVP!

We began on the second floor. Concerned with the fans that were running in the room, we decided to leave them be. It was extremely hot and we also hoped that the fans would work in the same way as "white noise" would. White noise is usually generated by a device that makes a droning noise that it is said to help spirits to be able to use the energy of the noise to communicate in our realm. Lucky for us, it did seem to work in this manner, for we got some great audio clips. I do have to admit, though, that it seems that the audio we recorded on the third floor was more numerous, and clearer. Later, I learned that the homeowners had asked that the spirits remain on the third floor so as not to frighten the children who live in the home. So needless to say, I find it interesting that these spirits do seem to follow the "rules." They only cheated a couple of times, and probably because we were encouraging them to come closer to us.

After we'd set up the equipment, I thought that Tara might like a bottle of water. In this clip, you'll hear me talking to Tara, telling her I was bringing her one (water).

Checking EMF levels in the basement of a private residence. *Courtesy Crystal Washington, WCG*

Then, seeing she already had a bottle of her own, I pretend to be flustered with her, and say that I came all the way up there! But of course, my lovely and talented team psychic was intent on her purpose, and didn't notice that I was joshing her. She immediately asks me, "What's in here?" as she points to a small door. I tell her that I can't reach to get in there. During our conversation a male voice states, *"I'm dying Luann, I'm dying!"*

RECORDING ● **Track 77**
[5 I'm Dying Luann I'm Dying]

As far as I can tell, he's already dead, but maybe it wouldn't be a good idea to tell him that! It is surely not Eric speaking at this time. I've worked with him many times and can recognize his voice easily. Besides that, he was in the basement at this point. He'd found himself attracted to the cellar for some reason. Being open minded, I've always thought it best to let people go with their instincts. Many times, the instincts of a good investigator pay off.

We spent some time in the attic where it was brutally hot. We had done some EVP work, and had checked around the attic, getting ourselves accustomed to the lay of the rooms. Sweating and uncomfortable, we decided to take a quick cigarette break. We weren't outside for long, and as we headed back in, a wonderful, and exceptional EVP was captured. As the trio of smokers, Eric, René, and I, came back up the stairs, a hauntingly sweet little girl's voice tells us, *"A stitch in time saves nine!"*

RECORDING ● **Track 78**
[5 Stitch In Time Saves Nine]

Toward the end, a motorcycle goes by, distorting the end of this EVP, but I do believe she says more. The amazing thing about this EVP is that both Tara's recorder, and mine, which I'd left sitting upstairs while we enjoyed our smoke, captured this EVP. Since recording it, I've often wondered if there was some kind of message in the EVP, or if it was just a little girl repeating a phrase she had learned during life. As mentioned, she does say more, but the motorcycle that goes rumbling by on the street in front of the house keeps her words from being understandable. I'm hoping that subsequent investigations will tell us more about the children here.

Our researcher, Debby, has a feeling that the female children we hear may be the deceased children of one of the past homeowners, Mary and Elizabeth. Only time will tell; we will have to do many more investigations to get to the bottom of who these spirits are, where they came from, and why they've connected to this home so strongly. I don't know if this little girl is Mary or her sister, Elizabeth, but I do know that her voice is haunting, and makes me wish that I could find a way to help her. This raises another question: Can the living actually help the dead? I'll never be sure if it is comforting to them when I acknowledge that I have heard them with the help of my recorder. Or if talking to us eases the pain that so many of them seem to feel, but I will keep trying. One can only hope for the best, so if I can't help them, at least maybe I can learn more about them through the use of audio recordings and the many tools we use on investigations.

Just after the *stitch in time* clip, and after the motorcycle passes, another EVP in the same voice, tells us, *"Daddy didn't come home!"* A woman's voice can also be heard just after the child telling us about her missing daddy. I did not include a loop of the woman's voice, since it is very soft; after practicing with the EVP on the *Dead Whispers* audio CD, you may want to try your hand at hearing it. I believe it says, *"Jack leave us!"*

RECORDING ● **Track 79**
[5 Daddy Didn't Come Home]

Again, both my recorder and Tara's recorder captured this. Tara was upstairs in the attic at this time, and that is where I left my recorder while we were outside smoking. Tara kept feeling a woman, who she thought was possibly in turmoil, and she wasn't sure if the children and this woman were related to each other, or if they were separate. An EVP that I did not include is of a woman screaming, just before Tara tells me that, "I keep hearing a woman screaming." This EVP made me think that it was possible the woman was related to at least one of the children. It could be that this man, "Jack," had left and never returned. So far, we have not found a record of a "Jack" associated with the house, but we also believe that, somehow, spirits are channeled to this house—be it an energy source, a high crystal quartz content, a vortex, or some other factor, we have not as yet discovered. As I've said before, this house has been difficult to trace because of the town line changes over the years, but we hope that at some point, we can identify at least some of the spirits that reside here in the afterlife.

Deciding to take some time on the second floor to cool off, we returned to the family room. It was still warm, but the fans helped to bring in some cooler night air. We spread ourselves comfortably about the room and began an EVP session. René was sitting closest to the teenage girl's bedroom and jumped up. She had seen a shadow move across the doorway of the girl's bedroom. She moved into the room to see what had caused the shadow. René never takes anything at face value and always tries to find a cause. She quietly moves about the bedroom, trying to find a source for the shadow. As she wondered out loud if it could have been a reflection from the cars moving by on the street outside, a male voice identifies himself as, *"George."* Both her recorder and mine recorded this name.

Track 80
[5 George]

Was George the shadow that René saw, and was he identifying himself? With this house, it might be impossible to find out, for we've begun to think that many of the spirits here are "floaters." By that, I mean that many of the ghosts came to this location from other places—they were attracted to this home for some reason. At this time, I can't say for sure if there is a "portal," which is what we think may be an opening between realities. With so many possibilities, it's hard to say why there are so many spirits here.

After we'd cooled off a bit, we decided to brave the heat in the attic. Tara and I settled ourselves in one end room. René decided to go alone into the other end room. There had been a video taken by Andrew Lake of Greenville Paranormal in which the door opened by itself. René closed herself into the room and shut the door. Turning off the light, she asked if the spirit(s) could walk by the door. The EVP captured is a whisper in the middle of this clip, *"I can't see nothing!"* (Not included.) At the end of the clip, she goes on to ask if they can sing a song.

Now, as long as I've been investigating, I'd thought on whether spirits could see in the dark or not. This clip makes me consider whether the spiritual body has the same failings as a living one does, and cannot see if there is no light. I have to admit, I have thought about in my time as an investigator if what a spirit *believes* has any effect on what they *experience*. For instance, if a spirit thinks it is still living, would it then feel the ailments and weaknesses of a human body, even in the afterlife? Or if they have specific religious beliefs, does that also affect what they experience as a ghost? Either way, I'm not ready to find out personally...yet!

Now, you've been to many places with me, and heard the voices of the dead as I've heard them. Every now and then, I have to admit that I hear an EVP that makes me cry, or feel so terrible for the frightened, traumatized lost souls that I have met. But once in a while, I hear an EVP that makes me laugh out loud! This next example of EVP is definitely one that gave me a good laugh. Tara and I were still in the end room, sitting, discussing the things that she felt as a psychic.

René had left her room on the end, and joined Eric LaVoie in the hallway. They were discussing one of the hall doors that wouldn't open, and had discovered that the door was stuck only because there was a large piece of furniture behind it. It hadn't been there the last time René had visited this home. The two of them were exploring the room, which was used by the family as a large closet/storage space.

Gabby and I are reflected well in this ornately carved mirror in a privately owned home.
Courtesy Crystal Washington, WCG

On further inspection, Eric and René noted some kind of animal excrement along the edges of the eaves where the roof met the house walls.

In the background, they are talking about this fact. Renés inaudible statement can be heard from the other room. But I remember hearing them speculating on if it was a rat, and mentioning that they should tell the homeowners about possible vermin in the attic. In the foreground, you'll hear me speaking to Tara from the end room. We're discussing one of the spirits and wondering together if maybe he doesn't come up to the third floor, "Unless it's not up here on the third floor." Tara agrees with me saying, "That's what I thought."

Behind our voices, a whisper, which sounds like a female voice to me, exclaims, *"Ah Jesus...they say a rat!"*

RECORDING ⏺ **Track 81**
[5 Ah Jesus They Say a Rat]

To me, it sounds like one spirit that says, "Ah Jesus," and another that exclaims, "They say a rat!" I can't help myself; I find it funny that even in the afterlife, some people are still afraid of rats!

After this initial investigation in this beautiful historic home in Acushnet, I found myself somehow attached to the spirits there. That child's voice ringing through the halls and the woman with her fright of rats somehow touched me. I thought about the possibility that the gentleman, who informed me by name, might be dying or re-living his death over and over. Could that be what has him stuck in this plane of existence? It seemed to me as if there was an invisible drama in this home, where a child and her mother waited endlessly for daddy to come home. Along with EVP, there seemed to be a whole world going on underneath our level of being, where we can only sometimes connect and hear voices call out to us.

I hope to continue investigating this home, and possibly learn more about these lost voices, these dead whispers that ring somehow into our realm, that break the barriers of death, and touch our hearts to the very core. For won't we someday leave behind this living existence? Won't we someday find ourselves on the other side?

CHAPTER SIX

LUANN'S HOME FOR THE WANDERING DEAD

"The Mother." *Courtesy Crystal Washington, WCG*

When we first started out here together, I hinted at my haunted life. But I do believe it's hard to understand if you've never been haunted. I didn't explain to you how often haunting things actually happened. I didn't tell you about the most recent investigation in which I tried to capture more evidence of the new spirit in my home. I didn't tell you how terrified my son, Tyler, and his girlfriend, Kara, were of this tall, dark, and not-so-handsome ghost man. Or that he not only peeped at me in my room without any clothes on, but he would tear the shower curtain open on Tyler when he'd take a shower here at my house. I didn't tell you that even I, hardened and conditioned after a lifetime of experiencing the paranormal, was afraid of this spirit for a time. I also didn't tell you that after doing some mini-investigations in my house that I am not so sure this ghost is even human anymore.

We first noticed activity in September of 2010, when a tall, black shadowy man would be seen walking in the house, or hovering over Tyler in his bed. Later, in October of that year, Kara, my son's girlfriend would sleep over while they were waiting for their own apartment. She began to complain of a black shadow that was shaped like a tall man being in her face when she awoke in the middle of the night.

Over the next several months, the activity got stronger, more frequent, and more violent.

On November 8, 2010, I had just finished writing for the day and had taken a shower. Wrapped in a towel, I entered my room to remove the towel from my body to wrap it around my hair. I sat upon my bed facing the mirror in my bureau. I was just about to open the drawers to pull out some clothes when I looked up to see reflected in my mirror, a tall, dark man walk across my bedroom on the other side of the bed. Seconds after that happened, I heard a plate rattle in the kitchen and thought that either Kara or Tyler, who were doing dishes, must have dropped a plate. I sat thinking about the apparition I'd just seen, and hoping that the kids hadn't dropped one of my antique plates on the floor.

Tyler came knocking at my bedroom door just then. He explained that he was checking for dishes that may have been left around the house. While he was at it, Kara was at the sink rinsing dishes before putting them in my dishwasher. Just as he came back into the kitchen, he saw something whiz by the corner of his eye to go crashing into a plate on the counter hard enough to make it rattle. When I went into the kitchen to examine the area, I found one of baby Logan's toy blocks that had probably been somewhere on the floor before it made its maiden flight. Not wanting to scare the kids, I thought to myself that it took quite a bit of force to throw a toy block hard enough to rattle a plate.

Two days later, I was in my bed reading a book. I heard a thump from Tyler's room and thought silly teenagers must be horsing around and one of them must have hit their head on the wall. The next thing I knew, I had two terrified teens in my room. They told me that something had somehow gotten water all over Kara and that the bed was soaked. They told me that they had heard something hit the wall.

Entering the room, I thought they had simply left a glass of water in the room and had somehow knocked it onto the bed. But on inspection, I found no glasses in the room. Even though Kara and the bed were wet, I could find no source for the wetness.

I began to speculate what I was dealing with. I had suspicions that it somehow related to the cult murder case that my team had inadvertently become involved with over the summer. Marvelous! A tall, dark man who believes he serves Satan! The sort of house guest you didn't invite, but likes to stay around.

Just before Christmas, on December 20, not a creature was stirring except maybe a ghost. I was asleep in my bed, with visions of sugarplums dancing in my head, when I was suddenly awakened by a terrible feeling that clutched around my neck. I have had this feeling before and I recognize it as the sign of a spirit that is nothing nice. As I lay in the darkness trying to gather my wits, wondering what had woken me, four black arms came coiling out of my pillow like snakes. I felt a cold grip around my wrists. Horrified, I pulled away from them, jumping out of my bed. When I turned to look back, the arms were gone. I knew I had seen them. I got up and clearly stated out loud that this spirit was not welcome in my home. Using the bathroom and determined not to be scared out of my own bed, I returned to my room—back to my bed, to lay down and sleep undisturbed for the rest of the night. In the morning light, I knew I had something in my house that I didn't welcome, and I considered just what I ought to do about it.

The next months were mostly quiet, with some small incidents of unexplained noises and small items being thrown around the house with force. As it all was happening I kept telling this spirit in no uncertain terms that it was not welcome here and that it had to leave. I knew that it was probably going to take considerable work on my part to get rid of this "man." I was also beginning to see a "cycle" to the activity, and this is why I always ask clients to begin a journal and log all the activity they notice. Time would go by without any activity and then, out of the blue, many incidents would happen all at once, around the same time.

It was becoming apparent that much of the activity was occurring around the full moon. I am not sure why this is true. Is it a coincidence that the night we were at Profile Rock, there was a full moon? Maybe spirits lack an energy source to keep activity up for long periods of time? Maybe the full moon's gravitational or magnetic pull on the earth helps them manifest activity? Maybe they are busy haunting someone else when they are not acting out in your home? Or possibly, they just have to have the right conditions at the right time to be able to manifest? Yes, we need more data, and more investigators to log and record.

Either way, things seemed to remain about the same for the next months. At times I would "feel" this presence, and other times, all would be quiet. The best I could do was to put up protections around my home and hope for the best. I knew that it would sooner or later come to a resolution and that I might be forced to face this thing in the end. The kids had moved out into their own apartment and I was enjoying freedom from motherhood for the first time. But, of course, I'd found that I wasn't really alone after all.

Lifelong habits are hard to break, and as is almost always the usual for me, I was in bed reading before I settled down to sleep. Turning the page, I noted a tall, dark, shadowy man materialize in the hallway and proceed to walk away, moving out of my view. Noticing my cat had woken out of a sound sleep to stare into the hallway, I watched as her head followed the apparition's movement across my doorway. Jumping down from the bed, she peeked around the door frame and possibly saw it advance further down the hall toward the kitchen.

Calmly, I told the man that he wasn't welcome here and that he needed to leave. Of course, he didn't listen again.

That was around the middle of May 2011, and by June, things had gotten much more active. Due to a plumbing problem in their apartment, Tyler and Kara came to stay with me for a few days. Retiring to my bed to read before sleep, I noticed that I was getting the all-too-familiar feeling around my neck. Hoping that if I ignored the creeping feeling it would go away, I let myself become absorbed in the story I was reading.

With hardly a knock on my door, Tyler came bursting into my room with his cell phone in his hand. "Look Ma! I got it on my camera!"

He passed me the cell phone and as I stared at its little screen, amazement took over. It looked as if he hadn't just captured it once, he had gotten it twice, and it seemed, in motion.

The next day I took the cell phone to the photo shop in Walgreen's Pharmacy and the clerk helped me to take the pictures off the phone. For the price of the cheapest memory stick they had and a picture CD, I finally had the man in my hands—well, in a sense at least.

Staring at this apparition, who at one point is so solid he looks human, something didn't seem right about the "man" I saw in the two separate shots. Knowing how many paranormal friends I have on my Facebook page, I decided to post them. Comments rolled in as I continued to study the photos. After Eric LaVoie of DART had changed the hues and contrast to make the images more clear, I realized I was looking at more than one ghost.

In the first picture, the kitchen is completely empty. Next, a tall man, with dark hair and clothing stands just to the left of my kitchen sink in front of the window. This "man" is solid enough to pass for a human. In the very next shot, two figures stand to the right of the window, or in front of where my dishwasher is located, facing each other. At first I thought the left-most figure was the same man who had been standing in front of the window in the previous shot. But this figure seemed to be wearing a dark hat and didn't seem as solid.

With the changes Eric, my para-brother, had made, I could now see that there were possibly *three* figures in this picture. In front of the window, where the man had first stood, it seemed to me that a small girl with dark hair had now appeared. Could

The apparition of a very angry spirit appears almost solid in the photograph taken in my kitchen. *Courtesy Tyler Harwood*

A second photo shows at least two more spirits are present in my home. *Courtesy Tyler Harwood*

that be Emily, the child spirit who has been in my homes for many years? If so, why was her hair dark in this picture? Everyone who had ever seen Emily saw her as a blonde. I knew she was blonde, for I had mistaken her for one of my two boys when they were younger. Both of them were very blonde when they were small enough for me to mistake Emily for them. And who in the world was the short, somewhat squat woman who stood in front of the apparition with the hat, that I took to be Rita, the motherly female spirit that has been attached to me since I was young? I didn't know I'd had a third female spirit around my home. For some reason, I didn't find it surprising.

Deciding that it was time to investigate matters in my home, I called Crystal Washington, who had been through something like this before in other homes I'd lived in and got her up to speed. Not only was she willing, she was enthusiastic about helping me out again. We made plans for her to come over on June 18, 2011, the following Saturday. Preparing for the investigation, I looked forward to possibly hearing from my two "regular" female spirits, and getting to the bottom of who my new and very naughty male ghost was.

Eric LaVoie came early during the afternoon the day of the investigation to let me borrow one of his spare cameras. I usually only run audio recorders, but for tonight, knowing I only had Crystal to run video, I thought it would be wise to have another camera in the house. Later, I was to find something else had noticed Eric in my house that day.

Crystal arrived around 9:30 p.m. and we immediately began set up. We ran a simple set up that night. Crystal used her handheld video camera to keep an eye on my kitchen and also used it to move about the house. I set up the infrared camera and TV so it had a clear view of the kitchen. I planned to keep the camera running through the night even after the investigation. I placed a Sony audio recorder on the kitchen table to remain stationary throughout the investigation. Using my RCA, I did smaller recordings that I could listen to immediately. I had observed Mike Marcowicz, "The EVP Man" doing this on investigations and thought it was a great idea I'd like to try. Using this method, you get to hear the EVP you've recorded much sooner than if you wait until a later date to review. Crystal ran her EMF detector and continued taking still digital camera pictures. I settled on one of my couches and let the spirits in the house know it was time to talk.

Wanting to know more about the female spirits who have been with me so long, I let them know that they could speak with me if they chose. As for the man who had been spreading fear to the kids in the house and peeping at me in my birthday suit, I commanded him to name himself and state his business in my home. After five minutes had passed, I shut the recorder off to upload the file to my laptop so I could review it immediately. The very first EVP sounds like a male whispering, *"I'm just trying s---."*

RECORDING ● **Track 82**
[6 I'm Just Trying S]

Wondering just what this spirit was trying, I placed the recorder in a different spot that I thought would get less interference from our equipment and turned it on. As I reviewed the recording, Crystal was beginning to have a battery problem that would last all night and would cost her most of the batteries she had brought for the night. As she replaced the batteries in her camera, I continued to question the spirits. I demanded that this new spirit identify himself. Seven minutes had passed and I again reviewed the recording. Within seconds of starting the recorder up, I had another positive result. This time, the EVP confused me, for it was a riddle to me. *"Return to Turtle Lane,"* spoken in a female voice. This was a place I'd never heard of.

RECORDING **Track 83**
[6 Return to Turtle Lane]

I found references to it online as a horse farm, a theater, and a maple farm. But I had never been to any of these places, so how could I "return" to them? As a brain storm came upon me, I reversed this EVP and found that it clearly said, *"Down, down by the church."*

RECORDING **Track 84**
[6 Down By The Church]

To this day I am left wondering if it could possibly be a place I'd visited and had some bearing on one of the spirits. As I've mentioned before, it is said that many times when recording a negative spirit, the EVP will also say something when the clip is reversed. I had known that this spirit wasn't exactly one of the good guys. Once again, I set the recorder down to do its job.

Pondering on whether I'd hear more from the female spirits, Crystal continued taking pictures around the house. She had just had another set of batteries drain and had returned to the living room where she'd left her bags with the spare batteries. Out of the corner of my eye I thought I saw a shadow flit by, and I mentioned it to Crystal. An EVP comes in just after I tell Crystal that I'd thought I'd seen something, "I am here!" (Not included.) Just after the EVP, Crystal lets me know she's going to try another set of batteries.

Not long after this, another EVP was recorded on the Sony in the kitchen. I think it was a slight misunderstanding on the spirits' part. While we were setting up our equipment, I had also been explaining to the new spirit how everything worked, and that he needed to state his business and leave my home in peace. The EVP makes me consider that the female spirits might have thought that I didn't want to hear from them on this night. "*She doesn't want us to go 'round here,*" is said in a whisper, in what I feel is a female voice.

Track 85
[6 She Doesn't Want Us To Go Round Here]

After recovering this audio clip from the Sony, running longer recordings that weren't reviewed until later, I was glad that shortly after that, I let Emily and Rita know that they were welcome to speak. Or to help me in any way they could. Crystal and I were in the living room at this point, and I can almost imagine these two females watching us. For me, it's profound; it seems as if no matter what I ask, the females at least are willing to cooperate. Even though our spirits seem to be separated by time, space, dimension, or some other such thing that we humans haven't thought of yet, these spirits remain good friends to me. Almost family.

Provoking the spirits is not something I normally do. I have always found that being polite and gentle gets me more responses. Feeling entitled to be a little angry with this male spirit, I think I had a right to provoke him a little. I called him names, such as coward, peeper, and pervert. I continually told him he wasn't welcome here. Just after that, an EVP chimes in that sounds like a young female, "*Entity!*"

Track 86
[6 Entity]

This EVP was also captured by the Sony recorder and sounds a bit louder. Could this be the voice of Emily, the child ghost that has been seen so many times in my home? If it is her, was this a warning that something was in my house? Since I already knew that something was in my house, I'm taking this as a friendly warning from the other side.

Crystal and I had been going at it for some time now. We decided it was time for some chocolate. I'd bought delicious frozen ice cream candy bars, and we snacked and enjoyed each others company. As sometimes happens with Crystal and I, we got a bit silly. In the recording you will hear Crystal using the old expression you might see from time to time on bumper stickers adorning custom vans, "If the van's rocking, don't come knocking," my voice chimes in with hers at the end, "Don't come knocking." I wonder if our dirty little jokes had stirred up something in one of the entities, for I find this a very strange expression, "*Virgin boy I can kiss.*"

Track 87
[6 Virgin Boy I Can Kiss]

132

But then again, if I'm right, I am dealing with the spirit of a dead murderer, and whatever he and his friends conjured up in the Freetown State Forest in the dark of night during Satanic rituals. At the same time, I feel threatened by this, for the only virgin boys that come around my home are my grandchildren. I can only hope and pray that I can rid my home of this new situation and that what I've read, that children have special protection from whatever powers may be, is true. I have enough faith in myself that by the time you read this book, my home will be entity free!

Getting serious again, Crystal and I settled back in to investigate. I was disappointed that the real problem hadn't been captured on the shorter EVP recordings I'd been making with the RCA and reviewing immediately. I began to let myself get a little angry again and called the spirit out. I felt justified in telling this thing to name itself and leave my home. I wasn't expecting a threat to anyone in my life.

Earlier in the day, Eric LaVoie, the founder of Dartmouth Anomalies Research Team (DART) had come by to drop off an infrared camera and recording device. He was in my home for a short time. Outside, under warm June sunshine, we smoked and caught up with each other on our cases. I didn't think much of his visit other than being happy to see him as I set about trying different areas where I'd like to set up the camera that night. But apparently, something else had noticed Eric's presence in my house.

Crystal asked me if I had left my door open and if it was easily closed by the wind from a window or anything. I told her that my door was hard to close because it rubbed on the rug. We spent some time working with the door, for as Crystal had stood taking pictures at the end of my hall, she saw my door close on its own. I know from experience that the high rug pile makes it impossible for anything to close the door in such a manner. I let Crystal work this out for herself, for this is why I invited her—to disprove anything she could and be my *devil's advocate* for the night. After asserting for herself that the door was not easily closed, she returned to the living room.

During the time that we were in the bedroom working with my door, the RCA in the living room picked up an EVP. "*New friend.....Eric,*" sounds as if it is two separate voices. (Not included.) "New Friend" sounds deeper and slower, while "Eric" sounds higher and faster. Over the years, I've heard many strange examples of the voices of the dead. At times their speech is hurried, much faster than we can understand. But once slowed down, can be understood better. Other times it is slower, or more than one voice may speak at once. In this case, I think it may be the same voice, but at different time rates. As I have time to work with this recording, I might be able to tell if it is indeed one voice. Soon after this EVP, I came closer to finding answers about the entity that was present in my home.

What I have come to believe is that during Whaling City Ghosts' stay in the dark woods of the Freetown-Fall River State Forest, something came home with me. More than one something. One or more of the murderers are deceased and I do believe at least one of them has graced me with his presence.

At the same time, I wonder, what exactly did they stir up out there in the woods? Were they really successful in calling something of an inhuman nature to this earthly plane? The next EVP makes me think just that. And that it is visiting my home on a regular basis, instilling fear in two teenagers' hearts. Is this *thing* responsible for much of the activity we've experienced in my home? Well, I have to wonder, and I have to listen to the voices I recorded in my home. I also have to try to do what's best for all concerned. I don't think it's a good thing to have a resident entity!

Returning to the living room to continue EVP work, I kept explaining in no uncertain terms that bad spirits and entities were not allowed in my home. I commanded it over and over to name itself, for as I have learned in the field, names are power. In a way, it has named itself and has given me a clue as to what I am dealing with. "*Defier....the beast,*" is what it calls itself.

RECORDING

Track 88
[6 Defier the Beast]

This voice is very deep, definitely male, and to me, very aggressive. As I later found out, he's also very possessive. Unless he's willing to start paying some rent, he'll find I'm a bit possessive of my home, too. Now, I'll admit any day, I do appreciate the spirits I've met in my lifetime. They have shown me just how fragile, and yet how tenacious the human soul is. In meeting, conversing, and feeling for the dead, I have come to appreciate life that much more. Life is a gift and we should all treat our lives that way. Not as a given, but something that can be torn from us at any time, without warning.

I chase after ghosts on a regular basis and encourage them to communicate with me. Occasionally, the price some investigators have to pay is that a spirit might follow them home. On rare occasions, something that was never human, and never will be enters the picture. Because I have past experience with this phenomena, it is more likely to happen to me again. And again.

Some in the field have told me I have a "calling." This means that it was meant for me to deal with these entities and that I have been called to do it. I don't know about that. What I do know is that I have had years of experiences, with both human and non-human entities alike. Though I do not enjoy experiencing the activity that these entities are usually associated with, I do look at it as a chance to study them. To bring the field forward and to understand how inhuman spirits are even possible. What I do know from experience could fill a book and I do plan on doing that in the near future. I also know that the only way we can come to understanding this type of haunt is to continue to study and document them. In the pursuit of this, I open my home and the EVP recorded there to you. I hope that by doing so, I help us all to understand these entities. With understanding, will come help for those who suffer from cases like mine. As I have said, they are extremely rare, but they do exist. They exist and at the time of this writing, one is here, interacting with the living. One who apparently considers me its property.

Crystal had settled in front of the windows in the living room to once again change her batteries. She'd had battery failure all night and was actually running low on batteries. She'd brought eighteen batteries with her. By now, she was down to four; it seemed very clear that something had been sucking her batteries of energy all night.

I had gone to find some of the baby blocks that he had thrown before and put them on the table in view of the cameras for him to throw again. Crystal told him he was a wimp and that he couldn't throw anything because he was too weak. As I was agreeing with her, something clattered on the floor next to Crystal. Getting up to investigate she found a strange screw on the floor by the entry door. Looking at the screw, I could not at first place it. Remembering my borrowed camera, I looked over the screws holding it on the tripod and found it identical. I found the remaining screws were tightly fitted and were not easily turned. I can not explain how the screw turned itself until it became unfastened and then ended up across the room by Crystal. I do know that when I set it up, I checked to make sure the screws were tight, as I didn't want the borrowed camera to fall and get damaged.

Before returning to the living room to check the RCA recorder for EVP, I checked the Sony that was running in the kitchen. During the night, I had stopped the Sony to begin recording again. I like when my recordings are not over an hour. It's much easier to listen to shorter recordings when it comes time to review them. My voice comes first stating that the Sony only had seventeen minutes so far, and I would leave it running. Shortly after that, a voice clearly calls me a "B—ch!" (Not included.) I find it very rude to call your hostess names in her very own home. I'm sure that this particular entity never went to a school of eloquence. I'm also sure that though I told this spirit that he was not welcome in my home, and told him to leave at the end of the investigation this night, he didn't leave.

Crystal was staying over for the night, but I knew she had early morning engagements, so by 1 a.m., I decided it was time to wrap up for the night. Before I ended, I told the entity again to leave, that I banished it from my home, and that it could never come back. For some reason, my demands were not met, and the entity chose to stay. Since I do most of my work in a non-denominational, sort of Native American way, I thanked the good spirits, Great Spirit, and my totem animals, and released them from my "circle."

Since I am writing this almost as it happens, I hope that by the time you read this, I have come to reconquer my home.

Crystal and I sat and spoke with Tyler and Kara before heading to our respective bed or couch to settle down for the night. In the morning, all seemed quiet, as far as the eye could see. But later in the day, I received an email from Crystal that she had heard something say, "Hi," to her during the night. I wasn't surprised, for things still didn't feel right in my home. My son, Tyler, was soon to attest to that.

Settling down in bed with a book, I wasn't expecting to hear from this spirit so soon. I'd only read a page or two when terrified teens once again entered my room. Kara was more upset than my son, but he has lived with ghosts ever since he can remember. They told me that they were preparing for bed when a tall, black apparition had appeared in their room. Kara said she swore she'd heard some type of words being whispered. Immediately, I got out of bed, grabbed my recorder and began to challenge this entity that seems to have a fetish for scaring kids. As I entered my son's room, I was determined to be much harder to scare.

None of us in the field know how these things work, or what weapons we possess to fight back with these darker entities. Some believe that our only defense against spirits of a darker nature is the Bible. I admit, I use the Bible frequently, but it is not my only tool. Many others in the field use sage to do a protective "smudging" in which the sage is burned and the smoke is used to protect and bless an object, place, or person. Still others will claim that religious artifacts, such as crosses, or holy water can help in a case such as mine. I use a combination of these things, but I also try new things, and I like to think that I have a few tricks up my sleeve.

When I first entered that room, ordering the kids into the living room to be out of my way for the time being, I let my "mother love" flow out of me to protect Tyler and Kara. I don't think there is any bond on earth stronger than the bond between a mother and her offspring. I was ready to rumble.

Earlier, I mentioned that provoking is not the usual way I do things. It's even against my nature in life to provoke. I try to tread gently through life and have found that ghosts respond to my personality. It's natural for me to converse with people who aren't there. I treat ghosts as if they are people. In my eyes, they were once human, deserving respect and care. Over the years, I've been richly rewarded for my actions. I've never counted all of the audio clips that I have recorded, but if I ever did, I'm sure it would be several hundred. Most of the EVP data in my archives are friendly in nature. Instances like "Dick" in the Dartmouth case are rare for me, and as I've explained, I think it's more that Dick has a problem with being dead than he does with me personally. He probably wasn't the nicest person in life either, if he has all the other spirits aggravated with him.

I've gotten to look in the eyes of some of my ghosts. And it has been with gentleness and care that human spirits have reached out to put an unseen hand on my physical body. But provocation is something I must do at times and in this case was warranted. This spirit had been told the "house rules" numerous times. House rules include not disturbing me in specific ways. An example is never to turn the lights on and off while I'm reading. Another rule is never, ever scare the children in the home. My son might be an adult now, but he's always going to be my child. I take offense to rule breakers in my home.

Closing myself into my son's room, I sat on the bed to make myself comfortable. I said a prayer to gather myself and my thoughts, and then I let that thing have it.

There are many things you can call an entity of this nature, so I did just that. One theme that I kept up with was telling it how weak it was and how little respect it deserved, since it preyed upon the young and inexperienced. I kept asking for help from the higher powers I believe in, and commanding it to name itself. As usual, in between my questions and commands, I gave time for it to answer me. With silence heavy upon me, it startled me to hear a strange voice inside the room. I wasn't sure what it had said, possibly the word "fine." Not knowing if maybe Tyler and Kara had crept up outside the doorway while I was concentrating on my audio session, I asked out loud, "What was that?" There was no reply. Getting up to check, I found both Tyler and Kara seated in the living room quietly awaiting the outcome of my session. Knowing I'd heard something in that room with me, I grabbed up the RCA recorder and hurried to listen to the audio.

In a matter of minutes, I heard the voice I'd heard in the room, but things weren't fine, as I thought I'd heard. The voice I'd heard was stating, *"You're mine."*

RECORDING **Track 89**
[6 You're Mine]

I was torn in two by this recording. Part of me was excited that I'd caught an auditory voice phenomenon with the recorder. The other part was offended that any entity thought it could call me its own. Quickly saving the clip, I returned to record more audio. This time I invited the kids into the room for I wanted to help them to help themselves a bit. Especially Kara. She had not grown up with paranormal activity surrounding her as had my son. I believe that people who are experiencing this type of activity must know that they can have power over their environment, and it starts with conquering their own fears. The kids joined me enthusiastically, partly excited to be included in my investigation. But I also think craving to face their fears. And to conquer them.

Sitting in the semi-darkness I began by showing them the way. I told this thing that I was not anyone's but my own. I told it that it was weak, and it had no power over me. Going on, I told it that this was my house, and it was not welcome here. Leave! Looking at Tyler, I told him to repeat after me. He repeated my words, telling it that it had no power over him. This is his mom's house and it had to leave. Turning to Kara, I followed the same monologue and she repeated after me. I made her do it again, with more power and you could almost see her confidence grow as she repeated the words. "This is Luann's house! You leave!" I couldn't have felt more proud of her than I did then. She has had the least experience with the paranormal, which for most people is normal.

Life has never been normal for my two sons. But you can't lay it all at my feet. I'm not the only ghost magnet in the family. My sons have inherited some of my traits. Well, all right, maybe they've inherited a lot of my traits!

At the end of our session, I grabbed their hands and said a prayer for them. Together we told the entity to leave and not to come back. Reading the Bible in each room, then smudging it with sage ended the night. Reviewing the audio brought only swears directed at us by name. We were offered sexual services and I possibly have an answer to a request to tell us its name. Most of these are Class B and C recordings. If I can bring them out better for you to be able to understand, I will be sure to include them on our website for you to hear.

Once we had finished discussing what had happened that evening, and the kids seemed more sure of themselves, we all settled back down to bed for the night. We slept peacefully until morning, undisturbed.

But after reviewing the audio and thinking on this case, what will happen when the next full moon lights the sky? For as I look over my notes in the journal concerning my case, and check the moon charts, I see a pattern developing. Most of the activity that has occurred was on or around the full moon. My instincts and experience with this type of haunt tells me that I will face this spirit again. At the time of this writing, I am preparing to do just that. Unfortunately, it usually takes time to clear a home of an unwanted spirit. Though I rely on science to investigate the paranormal, I'm going to have to rely on belief and "magic" to see me through this.

Isn't speaking to ghosts pushing the limits of what we know as reality? Is believing in myself, and using that belief in a series of actions, magic in itself? I was told a long time ago that we, living humans, have more power than we know, that we are mind, body, and spirit together in one package. That gives us power over our environment. In my own way, I believe it, and I find there is magic in that. Isn't a human soul, a thing of eternal life, unending and unexplainable magic? To me, magic is the science that we have not learned as of yet. Maybe someday, it won't be magic anymore; it will be science. For hasn't every good action we've made led to good things? Haven't the mistakes we've made led to consequences? Is it magic, or just the natural order of the universe? A universe we've barely touched upon? For me, the wonders and mysteries of today will become commonplace tomorrow. Or maybe humankind will never have the science. But we can still have faith.

The phenomena I'm experiencing in my home as I write this is commonplace and many have experienced it. Most in the field call the entities "shadow people." I've never had cause to think that these shadow people actually exist. I had surmised that they were not truly ghosts or the spirits of living people who have "crossed over" to the "other side." I had never experienced a shadow person haunting and did not have much to go on, except via the reports of others.

After having a taste of the activity a shadow person displays, I still feel the same way. I might be wrong, but I do not feel as if a shadow person deserves its own category. I think it is just another way in which an inhuman entity may appear to humans. Tall, black, scary...it's a good way to instill fear in a victim. Behind the scary shape that we see visually, I believe there is something else—something that we are very far from understanding. I also believe that by documenting my own case, and those of others, that we will come closer to understanding these things. I can promise that I will not stop looking and that I will keep an open mind. For you all should know, I believe in endless possibilities. This peeper and pervert, this dark "man" in my home who instills fear in everyone who experiences him—even me—does not have long to be in my home. But during his stay, he has, and will, provide me with more data, more evidence that these types of haunts do exist. I have hope that in the future, we will all know more about them. That through education comes understanding.

I personally don't know what death is, or how those who have experienced it can still touch us, communicate with us, be seen by us. I don't know if some of the answers that many of us in the paranormal world seek can only be found once we have crossed the barriers between life and death. If the answers can only be found in...the end.

AUTHOR NOTE

I'm happy to report that, with the help from some very special ghostly friends, my home has been cleared of the negative entity that called itself "Defier the beast."

TIP

Negative entities are unknown, unproven, but still considered dangerous. If you do decide to start paranormal investigations, take the time to learn the risks. Do use protection and research the different types available – choose the one that fits your beliefs. Do research the areas you're covering and keep to haunts that have a more "positive" reputation. If you ever think you have been in contact with, or are being affected by, a negative entity, do find experienced help. Don't panic, don't feed into it; you are not alone. Reach out; do some research and find the right people in your area. If you can't find help, look for the contact information at the end of this book. I'd be glad to put you in contact with someone close by who can help you!

CHAPTER SEVEN

THE OTHER SIDE

"Stand Alone." Courtesy Crystal Washington, WCG

Massachusetts is known for having more cemeteries than any other state in America. While driving down any country road in southeastern Massachusetts, you will pass numerous small graveyards. Though we have large cemeteries that boast beautiful and ornate statuary, most of our graveyards are small family plots.

When this country was young, the people were spread out over large masses of land. It would have been a hardship to transport a body to a town or village for burial. Many of these small plots are so old that the slate headstones have eroded and the names and dates can no longer be read. Many others are long forgotten. You could be hiking through the woods and find yourself walking among tombstones. Other small burial grounds, such as the black cemetery (lost to time and without a name or specific location) in Dartmouth, Massachusetts, and many Indian burial grounds have been built over and forgotten. Walking through one of these plots surrounded by headstones and weeds, many of the names on the stones are prominent names in the history of this area, and some are forgotten families that no one has ever heard of and no living survivors remain. At times, you find yourself surrounded by entire families—father, mother, and a number of children—and you can't help but think about what happened to them...and who was left to bury their remains.

In later years, tuberculosis was rampant in the area. Large families succumbed and the stones tell their story. In Rural Cemetery of

Burials in Massachusetts can be a family affair.
Courtesy Crystal Washington, WCG

New Bedford, Massachusetts, many sea captains and their families are in their final resting places. Tiny headstones such as "Little Timmy" show where small children were interred. If you listen very carefully, you can almost hear the moans and sobs of their mothers, who lost them much too early in life. No matter where you are, in a larger public cemetery or a small family plot, you can't help but feel the history in these final resting places of the inhabitants of this area. And sometimes, you feel the ghosts who once walked these lands.

Tim Weisberg, Matt Costa, and Matt Moniz broadcast *Spooky Southcoast* every Saturday night, running a chat room in which you can listen to the show live online while interacting with not only the hosts, but some big names in the paranormal field. I visit as often as I can, not only to show support for the show, but because many of the fans have become friends to me. It is a good chance to chat about the paranormal while at the same time interacting with intelligent people about ideas. Countless times, I have found theories swirling through my head after chatting with the fans on *Spooky TV*. I've also found myself surprised when I've followed leads given to me by Spooky chatters. This next story is an example of just that.

Chatting away happily with the other members of the chatroom, one of them who calls himself "Standing Stones" started relating information about a place that he thought involved me in some way. His description seemed familiar, but at first, I could not place it. When he said something about a wheel in the distance, it made me think of a certain location I'd visited—a cemetery to be exact. Thinking I may still have a picture of the spot to show Standing Stones to see if he could identify it, I began searching my files.

On viewing the picture, Standing Stones was sure that it was the place. He thought that the site had a relation to me and that the key ghost in this scenario had the surname "Pritchard." I was intrigued by what he told me, and decided that as soon as I had time, I'd return to Dartmouth, and the edge of the state forest to see for myself.

Family members were left behind to look toward Heaven for their loved ones. *Courtesy Crystal Washington, WCG*

At times you find trees older than the gravestones adorning New England cemeteries.
Courtesy Crystal Washington, WCG

It was a beautiful autumn day when I finally had time to venture out to the cemetery Standing Stones had described. With sunlight shining at a long angle through the trees, it was a magical day to take photographs. I found myself wandering the area close by the cemetery just to take pictures and enjoy the day. Finally, I drove to the final destination of some of the inhabitants of Dartmouth. I took note of the field behind the cemetery, seeing the changes in it that Standing Stones had described. Taking some time to clear debris from around the stones, many of which were broken down to the bases, I enjoyed the stillness of the place. Even the crickets sang gently, reverent of this day.

I settled down on the base of one gravestone and set up the "Hack Shack" which, as I've explained earlier, is very like the Frank's Box device. (It uses a radio signal to help pick up words that are supposedly the voices of ghosts using the frequencies to help them communicate with the living.) I had only just begun experimenting with this device that Eric LaVoie of DART had donated to us and wasn't sure how well it worked. That day, it just seemed like the right tool to bring.

Asking questions and listening carefully through the headphones attached to the Hack Shack, I tried to filter out what I knew to be radio stations. Staring up through the branches that surround this old graveyard, I thought I heard words that weren't the radio, and in particular, I was sure I'd heard the name, *"Pritchard."*

Track 90
[7 Pritchard]

An angel touches down to grace this final resting place. *Courtesy Crystal Washington, WCG*

I craned my ears to hear more, knowing that my recorder was making sure I'd have the audio to go over later to verify what I thought I'd heard. Taking a small break, I sat and enjoyed the perfect New England weather and let my ears recuperate from the beating they take when listening to a Hack Shack. For a moment, I just watched the birds flying overhead and enjoyed my view of the farm next door to this place of memories long forgotten.

Finding a slightly more comfortable position on my seat of stone, I started the recorder up again and fitted the headphones to my ears. Blurbs of radio flashed by and then a sentence, longer than possible with the channels flowing by the way they do. It was too quick for me to pick up in its entirety as it streamed past my ears. I speculated what it had said—*something about coming back here*, I thought to myself. I couldn't wait to get home to review it. I stayed a while longer, asking questions and hoping to hear that same voice again. It was getting late, and I had to meet my son at home. I packed up and went home to review my audio.

The next clip you will hear is probably the longest Hack Shack recording I've ever heard. At the same time, I thought about whether this was the Pritchard person? And did he have some sort of message for me? I'm not sure... Maybe I'll let you be the judge of that, but I do know the answer in my own heart. You see, this clip asks me a question, that at the time, I was pretty sure I knew the answer to. Now, after even more adventures in the paranormal field, I'm *sure* I know the answer. For what he asks me is this: *"Before you come back here...was it all worth it?"*

Track 91
[7 Before You Come Back Here All Worth It]

Looking back on all I've done, all I've experienced, all the spirits I have met, I have to say it was well worth it. With each case, each spirit from beyond, I have learned something about myself. I have learned to look beyond what we can see as humans. I have learned to look differently at everything we all experience in our daily lives. I've found that what we put so much value in really matters little in the greater scheme of things. Each moment of our lives matters—for life is a gift and an experience that all human beings endure for a time. Do we all end being ghosts? Do some of us go on to another place, such as Heaven? Are we reincarnated again and again, as some say, until we've learned the lessons we require here on the Earth plane? What matter is our limited view of the lives we live when faced with endless possibilities?

Cold winter winds have twisted the form of this old tree. *Courtesy Crystal Washington, WCG*

Still, I can not give you answers, only guesses. There are no experts in this field and I can not claim to be one. Yes, I have experienced more ghostly activity than most, but when I look at the question, I have to say, yes, it was all worth it. I can only hope that for you, it was all worth it, too!

The next EVP is one that I can not explain, but for some reason always gives me a terribly creepy feeling when I listen to it. This clip was recorded in a building in the town of Fairhaven, Massachusetts. The location was once the home of the Wampanoag, long before the white man came to these lands, when they were still considered a "Woodland Tribe" and had not had any known contact with visitors.

Later, a massacre occurred in retaliation to the white men for killing all the women and children in a Wampanoag village. Still later, swampy land close by was filled in with possibly contaminated mill dirt. Even later still, very near to this site, a murder by stabbing occurred after a horrifying chase. Or at least it must have been horrifying to the victim, for it resulted in his death. A huge fire took out a large area of homes and buildings not far from the present site of this building. We are not sure if there were any casualties in the fire, as Debby is still working on the research to this case. It seems the more she looks into this site, the more she finds. Close by, runs the Acushnet River, the site of a severe PCB contamination and a super fund site. Along with that, the Fairhaven Bridge, which connects Fairhaven to the city of New Bedford was completely destroyed six times during hurricanes, or "gales" as they were known to be called in the old days. After some of these hurricanes, bodies washed upon the shores of the Acushnet River after being overtaken by waves or flood. The body of an unidentified woman was found on October 30, 1996, at Pope's Island, just a stone's toss across the water from this haunt. In this location, there's a chance for a wide variety of spirits to be kicking around. This vicinity also leaves open the possibility of more sinister behavior that went on in secret.

Whenever I listen to this clip, I have the shivery feeling that someone was not being nice to a child. I can't say exactly why I feel this way. It's something about the way it's worded. This is not a father telling the child, "Hush now go to sleep," this is a male telling a child, *"Little brat, keep those eyes closed."*

RECORDING **Track 92**
[7 Little Brat Keep Those Eyes Closed]

For some reason, I think there was bad intent behind the words. I'm a parent; I've been frustrated with my boys at times. Never would I call them little brats—little beasts maybe, but that was a joke in our family. Since I can't get past the feeling of bad intent that I feel when I listen to this clip, I'll leave it up to you to decide what this man meant when he whispered into the dark hallway of this old and haunted building. Was it just a father, after a long and frustrating day with his overactive child telling them to keep those eyes closed and get to sleep? Or was it something more sinister? We do have dates planned in the near future to investigate this building again. I hope sooner or later I'll get to the bottom of this strange recording. I promise, if I do, I'll let you know!

During our last investigation at this site in Fairhaven, Massachusetts, we recorded an EVP that I believe may relate to the fire Debby found in the history of the area. It brings chills to the spine hearing the words, *"Put us out!"*

RECORDING **Track 93**
[7 Put Us Out]

Dying in a fire has always been frightening to me, but even more frightening is to think that I would feel the pain and horror of the flames still licking at my body even after death. With all my heart, I hope this isn't the case for this female spirit, for I can't imagine anyone deserving such torture in the afterlife.

We have begun to suspect that there may be a mass grave close to this site, relating to the bodies that washed up during past hurricanes. What is not commonly known is that mass graves weren't such a rarity in history. Large numbers of dead bodies were next to impossible to identify since dental records were unknown at the time. Another factor was that there were no embalming practices until more modern days. If these bodies weren't buried quickly, the smell would have been horrible.

This next EVP makes me believe even more strongly that it is possible that a mass grave may be located very close to this property. Due to the wet conditions next to the river, I'm sure even the bones have decomposed and it may be impossible to ever know for sure. *"Find us!"*

RECORDING **Track 94**
[7 Find Us]

I know that we won't stop working on this case, or chasing down the history until we come closer to answers. I hope that soon, we can "find" the ghosts that are asking us to find them. These voices seem so desperate to me; I hope we can find a way to help them, to set them at ease, to find peace in the afterlife.

The next EVP still has me stumped. I have no idea what he means, and wonder if Bob is the inter-dimensional travel agent from the other side. *"To our destination call Bob, Bob, Bob!"*

RECORDING **Track 95**
[7 To Our Destination Call Bob Bob Bob]

Not able to make sense of this weird EVP, I got a brainstorm and reversed it. Suddenly it made more sense, though I am unsure if this is the truth. Reversed, the EVP says, *"Bob, Bob, Bob, shivved the girls."*

RECORDING **Track 96**
[7 To Our Destination Call Bob Bob Bob Reverse]

As we've discussed prior, the problem with an EVP that can be reversed, and still be understandable, is that this is usually the sign of a negative spirit. With so much history behind this site, we can only guess that some of the spirits here are not exactly positive. With such a maze of history and ever-changing land developments, we must wade through the paperwork and records in hope that we come close to answers.

What I find interesting here is the word "shiv" itself. Shiv is a slang prison term that means knife. Did a convict murder women here? Are the bodies of the women what the previous EVP refers to? Do the victims want to be found? Yes, once again, I have to say it—more research and investigation needed.

Some day, we may have answers to the questions that we ask as we delve into the world of the paranormal. Right now, and in the days to come, we are on the edge of new discoveries, new ways of doing things, new ideas. I believe it's only a matter of time before we get closer. Unless we are willing to go the extra mile, to think outside the box, and to be willing to try new things, we can still only guess at what the dead are saying to us. We labor toward that time, looking for the right conditions for the dead to tell us more. We can only reach out, waiting for them to reach back to us.

So, look beyond what you see every day. Question your vision and reach out into the unknown. I know that I wouldn't be where I am today if I hadn't stepped out beyond my own visions, reached out to listen to the dead whispers of the past. To hope beyond hope that what I have learned and what I think I know will carry me far when I reach the other side...

TIP

Most cemeteries are open from dawn to dusk. Many of them don't mind photographers or investigators visiting during normal business hours. Some locations even allow entry at night, by calling ahead and seeking permission. Always be respectful; never leave behind anything that wasn't already there, except maybe a footprint.

FINAL RESTING PLACE

The end of our journey together is near. I've taken you to many of my favorite haunts of New England, and invited you into my own home. You've heard the dead whispers of the ghosts that are near and dear to my heart. I hope that, along the way, you've not only learned to hear EVP but that you've also taken something with you. Chasing ghosts all over New England has changed my life and made it richer, fuller, more exciting, but also more valuable to me. I have watched people I love pass away, but I think I just might see them again. That rather than being sad that they are gone, I try to be happy that I will join them some day when it is my time to leave this plane of existence. I hope that by never letting myself stop learning, by questioning and trying new ideas that I have inspired you to do the same.

Whether you take up paranormal investigation as a hobby, or join it as a serious endeavor, take the time to enjoy what you do. We never have all the answers, we never know when our last moment of life will be. So, please take each one and live as if it were your last, for we never know when we might be the ghost left behind, desperately trying to communicate with the living.

With more experimentation and sharing in the paranormal field, I do believe there are good things for us to learn coming in the future. Join us here if you dare, or sit back and question what you see. For every question only makes us in the field work harder to find answers to the mysteries that lay before us on the other side.

As for me, I do believe in ghosts. I hope after reading and listening to the voices of the ghosts of New England, you come that much closer to believing, too!

Now that we have come to our final resting place, I'd like to invite you to visit us at whalingcityghosts. net and enjoy bonus EVPs and additional pictures from the locations discussed in this book. Don't be shy, make yourself at home!

Remember the tips I've given you and take your time with the EVP. The more you practice the better you become at listening to the voices of the dead. Meet the team and interact with us, we're all looking forward to meeting you!

Some of the video footage I've mentioned in this book can be seen at DART's website, dartparanormal. com. I'm sure you'll find Eric LaVoie's website not only interesting, but welcoming! Lizzie Borden video footage and show archives can be found at spookysouthcoast.com. You can also join the Spooky Crew every Saturday night from 10 p.m.-12 a.m. at their chatroom found on the "Live Show" link on their main site.

Of special note: The anomaly pictures in the book can be seen more clearly on our website, so don't be a stranger!

Look to the future and the answers tomorrow will bring. Never stop questioning the world around you and seek beyond what you think you know today. Who knows what one person can learn and bring into the light of our modern day? Who knows where our dreams may lead?

I hope that you've enjoyed your stay with Whaling City Ghosts as much as we've enjoyed having you with us!

Soon I hope to take you on another journey. Into the darkest of dreams......

RESOURCES

ACUSHNET HISTORICAL COMMISSION
122 Main Street
Acushnet, MA 02743
(508) 998-0200

DARTMOUTH ANOMALIES RESEARCH TEAM (DART)
Eric LaVoie/Founder
www.dartparanormal.com

DARTMOUTH HISTORICAL COMMISSION
400 Slocum Road
Dartmouth, MA 02747

FALL RIVER VISITOR INFORMATION
www.fallriverma.org/

FAIRHAVEN TOURISM OFFICE
www.millicentlibrary.org/tour_of.htm

FREETOWN-FALL RIVER STATE FOREST/PROFILE ROCK
Slab Bridge Road
Assonet, MA 02702
(508) 644-5522

GREENVILLE PARANORMAL
Andrew Lake
www.greenvilleparanormal.com

LIZZIE BORDEN'S BED & BREAKFAST
230 Second Street
Fall River, MA 02721
(508) 675-7333
Tours run from 11 a.m. to 3 p.m.
Rooms are available by reservation

MIKE MARKOWICZ
The EVP Man
www.evpmike.com

NEW BEDFORD WHALING
NATIONAL HISTORIC PARK VISITOR CENTER
33 William Street
New Bedford, MA 02740
(508) 996-4095

ROCKAFELLAS
231 Essex Street
Salem, MA 01970
(978) 745-2411
www.rockafellasofsalem.com

THE SALEM INN

7 Summer Street
Salem, MA 01970
(978) 741-0680
www.saleminnma.com

SALEM, MA

Visitor Information
salem.org

SPOOKY SOUTHCOAST

www.spookysouthcoast.com
Airs Saturday nights 10 p.m. – Midnight

WHALING CITY GHOSTS

www.whalingcityghosts.net